KU-195-939

Preface

We expect many things to move, but not the earth!

How could the earth, which is strong enough to support a skyscraper, shake and break up? Where do earthquakes come from? Are we ever going to know *when* and *where* they will hit? And could we ever learn to build structures capable of withstanding earthquakes?

Many years have passed since humans first experienced earthquakes. Over time, we have learned answers to most of these questions—but not all of them.

The book is built around projects, demonstrations, and simple experiments that make it easy and fun to develop a physical understanding of earthquakes and their natural relatives—volcanic eruptions and tsunami waves. You will enjoy working on most of these projects alone or with a friend; for a few, you may want to ask a parent or an older sibling or friend to help you. In either case, you will have a good time and also learn a lot about earthquakes, volcanoes, and tsunamis.

We hope you will enjoy reading this book as much as we did writing it, but above all, we hope that you will never meet face-to-face with an earthquake, an erupting volcano, or a tsunami.

NOTE: Although English units of measurement (feet, pounds, etc.) are still commonly used in the United States, almost all the other countries in the world have adopted a measurement system called the *metric system* or *SI*. This system is taught in our schools and is the official measurement system of our federal government. For these reasons, all the measures in this book are given first in metric units, then in the equivalent measures in English units.

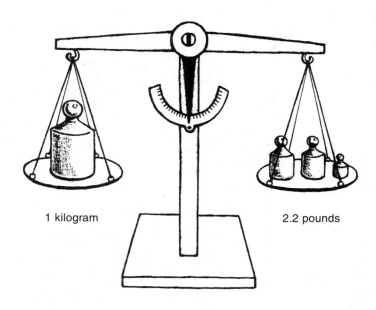

1 kilogram   2.2 pounds

3.28 feet = 1 meter

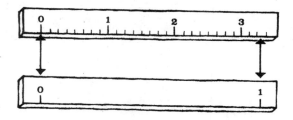

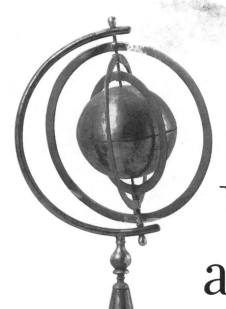

Earthquakes, Volcanoes, and Tsunamis

Projects and Principles for Beginning Geologists

MATTHYS LEVY AND
MARIO SALVADORI

CHICAGO
REVIEW
PRESS

Library of Congress Cataloging-in-Publication Data
Levy, Matthys.
    [Earthquake games]
    Earthquakes, volcanoes, and tsunamis : projects and principles for
beginning geologists / Matthys Levy and Mario Salvadori.
        p. cm.
    Includes index.
    Originally published: Earthquake games. New York : M.K. McElderry
Books, c1997.
    ISBN 978-1-55652-801-9
1. Earthquakes—Juvenile literature. 2. Volcanoes—Juvenile literature.
3. Educational games—Juvenile literature. I. Salvadori, Mario, 1907-
1997. II. Levy, Matthys. Earthquake games. III. Title.

    QE521.3.L486 2009
    551.2—dc22

                                                        2008040143

Cover and interior design: Scott Rattray
Interior illustration: Christina C. Blatt
Cover photos: iStock

First published in 1997 by Margaret K.
McElderry Books as *Earthquake Games*

This edition published by Chicago Review Press, Incorporated
814 North Franklin Street
Chicago, Illinois 60610
ISBN 978-1-55652-801-9
Printed in the United States of America
5 4 3 2 1

To the children of P.S. 45 in the Bronx, New York,
who first asked,
"Mario, how do earthquakes work?"
And to
Nicola, Okna, Shae, Edison, Austin, Daniel, and Maia

M. L. and M. S.

Contents

The Secrets of the Earth

We all live on the surface of the earth, but did you ever wonder what goes on beneath the surface, deep inside the earth, deeper than the deepest mine? No human being has ever been down there, but earth scientists have been able to learn a lot about what it's made of and what goes on inside the big sphere on which we live. And at the same time, their discoveries have helped to explain much of the mystery of how earthquakes happen and volcanoes erupt.

Imagine that the earth is like an apple or a peach and consists of a skin, a "meaty" part, and a core or pit. The *core* of the earth is solid metal (iron and nickel) surrounded by hot liquid metals. The

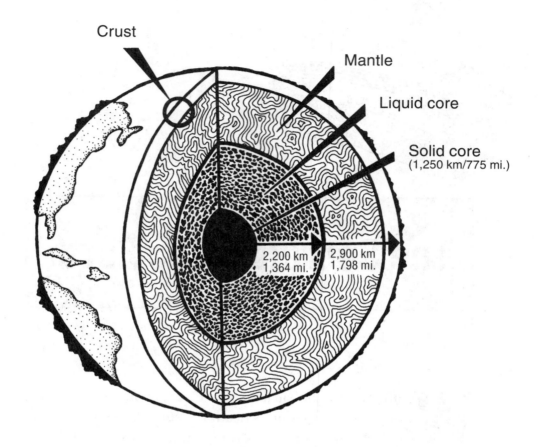

Crust

Mantle

Liquid core

Solid core
(1,250 km/775 mi.)

2,200 km
1,364 mi.

2,900 km
1,798 mi.

"meat" of the earth, the *mantle,* is a hot, somewhat soupy mass of melted rock called *magma.* The skin of the planet is its *crust,* the hard surface of the earth on which we live.

The crust is not equally thick all around the earth. It is as deep as 40 kilometers (25 miles) under the surface of the continents and as thin as 5 kilometers (3 miles) under the ocean floor.

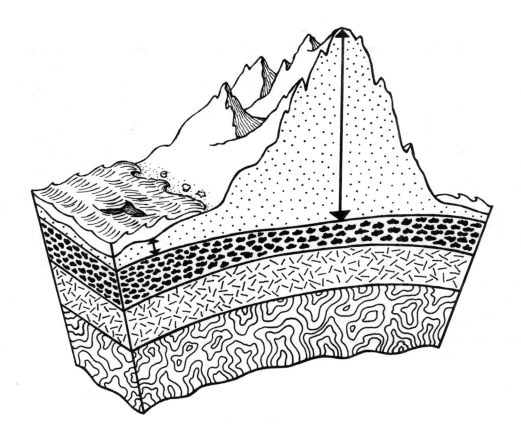

Until recently the crust was assumed to be solid rock, but discoveries have shown instead that it is cracked into separate sections called *tectonic plates*. Some of them are so large that they determine the boundaries of entire continents or oceans—one of the plates supports all of the United States, and the whole Pacific Ocean sits on another. Other sections are smaller, supporting only part of a continent or a small group of islands, like the plate under the Caribbean.

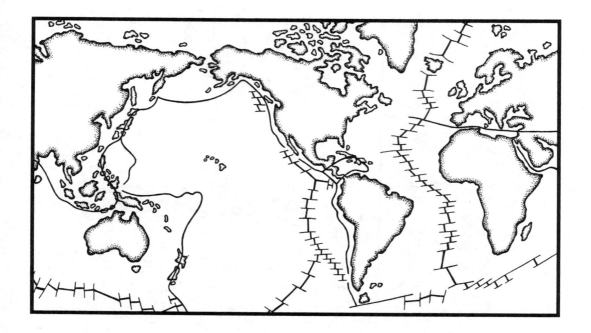

The Cracked Egg

In this experiment you will use a boiled egg to simulate the behavior of the tectonic plates on the earth's surface.

You'll Need

► adult helper
► cooking pot
► water
► egg
► spoon
► clock or timer

1. Put enough cold water in a pot to cover an egg. With the help of a parent or other adult, bring the water to a boil.

2. Lower an egg into the boiling water with a spoon. Turn the heat down to a low boil and cook the egg for about 7 to 9 minutes.

3. Take the egg out of the water and cool it under cold water. The egg should be medium cooked, not hard.

4. Strike the boiled egg gently against a hard surface, like the top of a kitchen table, and break the eggshell into a number of pieces, some large and some small. They will be the tectonic plates of your "earth."

5. If you now squeeze the egg gently between two fingers, the "plates" will move. Some will bump against adjoining plates, others will slide along them, and some will move away from each other. A plate may even slide under an adjoining plate.

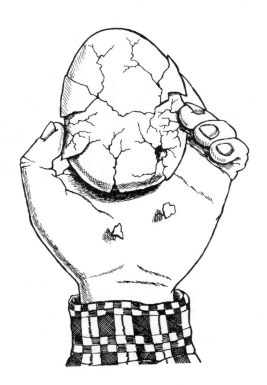

NOTE: Since the consistency of a boiled egg varies depending on its age, the suggested boiling time is approximate and you may have to proceed by trial and error to be successful with this experiment.

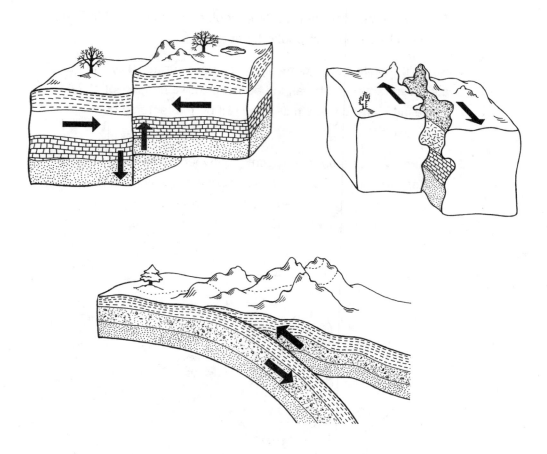

Just like the pieces of the eggshell in the egg experiment, the separate tectonic plates floating over the magma don't stay put but move around at a snail's pace, at only 50 millimeters (2 inches) a year. As they move toward each other, one plate may hit another (top left), slide along it (top right), or even duck under it in a movement called *subduction* (bottom).

Scraping Plates

To feel how the tectonic plates bump into each other and create earthquakes that damage buildings and kill people, you only need to use your hands.

You'll Need
▶ 2 hands

1. Make your hands into fists with the knuckles bulging out. The backs of your hands will be your "plates" and the knuckles will represent the rough "edges" of the tectonic plates.

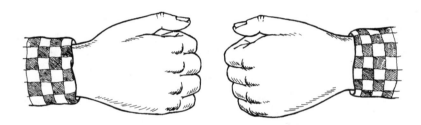

2. Push your knuckles together, and at the same time try to make one hand slide with respect to the other. The harder you push your knuckles together, the harder it will be to make your hands slide; you will feel the stress increase along your knuckles, just as it increases between the rough edges of the plates.

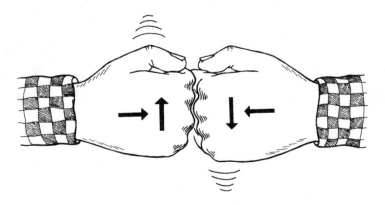

3. If you keep pushing for a while, the muscles of your "plates" will start hurting because the knuckles are preventing the sliding. But eventually one "plate" will suddenly slide, releasing the energy accumulated in your hands. This is how an earthquake happens.

From the time our planet first came into being about five billion years ago, somewhere on earth two plates under the continents have bumped and pushed against each other, neither of them giving in; they pushed and pushed, and eventually bent up the earth's crust. This is how they created high mountains—and still do.

The Birth of Mountains

You can feel how mountains form through this demonstration.

You'll Need
▶ 2 hands

1. Keep your hands flat, with palms down, and push your middle fingers against each other, tip to tip.

2. Your hands represent the tectonic plates. If you keep pushing your hands toward one another, you will feel the energy stored in them. If you then make one hand slide under the other in a "subduction," the stored energy will be released, generating an "earthquake."

3. But if you keep pushing harder and do not slide one hand under the other, your fingers will bend up, creating "mountains." The middle fingers form the highest mountain; call it Mount Everest (or, by its Tibetan name, Chomolungma, Goddess Mother of the World). It is the highest mountain on earth, at 8,848 meters (29,029 feet) high. Your ring fingers in this experiment represent the second-highest mountain, K2 (or Godwin Austen), which is 8,611 meters (28,251 feet) high. Your index fingers form Kanchenjunga, the third-highest mountain on earth at 8,598 meters (28,209 feet) high.

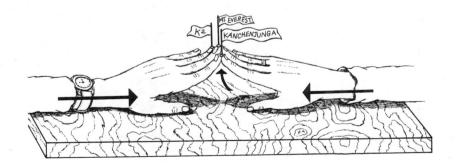

NOTE: The height of these three mountains is actually increasing yearly by several millimeters as the Indian plate pushes against the Eurasian plate.

Along the plate boundaries where one plate dips below another, such as where the Pacific plate dips beneath the North American plate, the edge of the lower plate plunges down into the incredibly hot mantle and melts. If a crack already exists in the crust at that point, the pressure from the weight of the crust pushes up the boiling hot melted rock, the magma, through the crack. This is how a volcano is created. Because the earth's crust is so much thinner under the oceans, many more volcanoes are generated there than on the surface of the earth.

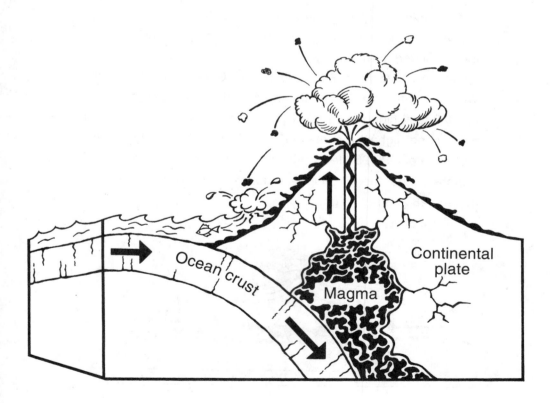

When two tectonic plates move away from each other, also most often at the bottom of the ocean, a crack opens in the earth's crust through which magma is squeezed up in volcanic eruptions, creating a series of underwater mountains called *ridges*. The one place on earth where this kind of crack passes through land and you can actually see these ridges being born is on the island of Iceland.

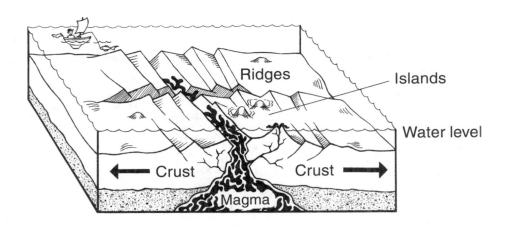

Ever since the earth's crust hardened, earthquakes have occurred, not all over the earth's crust but mainly along the edges of the tectonic plates. The most active earthquake areas are along the rim of the Pacific Ocean, called the *circum-Pacific belt*, which starts in Japan and circles the Pacific Ocean, bringing devastation to Alaska, the West Coast of the United States, and South America, as well as Southeast Asia. Earthquakes also occur along a strip from Portugal to Australia cutting through Italy, Greece, Turkey, and Iran, called the *Alpide belt*.

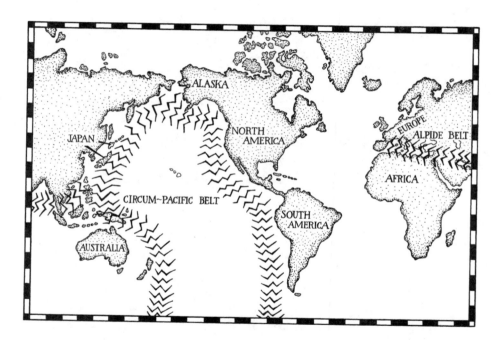

Falling Towers

To show how earthquakes can damage buildings and kill people, try this demonstration.

You'll Need

▶ 8 wooden cubes

▶ helper

1. Have your helper erect two towers, with three or four wooden cubes each, on the back of one or both of your hands.

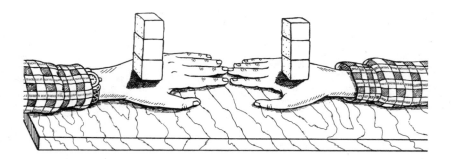

2. Push your hands together as you did in the Birth of Mountains demonstration (see p. 9) and suddenly let them slide against each other. The cube towers will likely collapse.

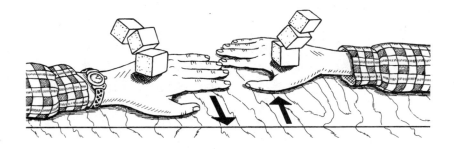

3. Imagine that the towers were actual buildings resting on tectonic plates. How devastating can an earthquake be?

Some earthquakes are weak and do not do too much damage, but the worst can destroy entire cities and kill thousands upon thousands of people. The most deadly ever, which struck Tangshan, China, in 1976, killed more than three hundred thousand people.

At the present time, most of the residents of the United States are lucky: strong earthquakes and volcanic eruptions occur mainly on the West Coast. But in the past there have been deadly earthquakes in the East and in the Midwest, as the dots on the map below show.

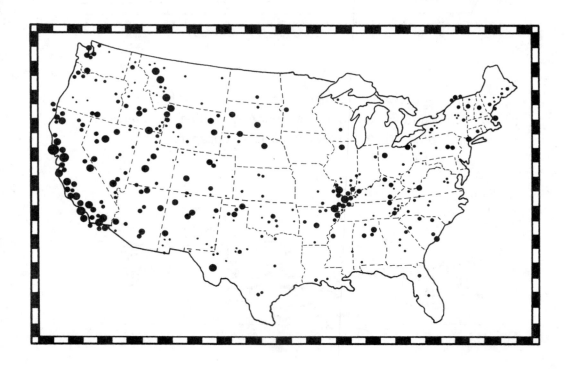

Questions

1. Since nobody has been inside the earth, which is so hot that whoever tried would be burned to death, how can we know so much about it?

When two tectonic plates hit each other in a subduction, they send out "signals" called seismic (earthquake) waves, which can be "heard," just as we can hear the sound waves from a faraway explosion. Because the waves travel at different speeds through the different materials that make up the earth (see chapter 4), listening to the seismic waves has allowed earth scientists to determine what those materials are.

2. I have heard that the continents move over time. Will we, anytime soon, be able to walk from the United States to France?

Not unless you plan to live a long, long time! But you are correct—the continents are believed to once have been all joined together as one big continent called *Pangaea*, which then cracked. The sections (our present continents) drifted apart and are now beginning to move together again. If this movement continues for another 200 million years, the continents will be close enough to build a bridge between New York City and Lisbon, Portugal.

3. If the tectonic plates are floating on the soupy magma, wouldn't they tilt if we built all of our cities on one coast?

No, the earth's crust is so heavy that what we build on it is like a fly on an elephant. But, as a matter of fact, the continents do tilt over time as the tectonic plates push against one another. The North American continent tilts toward the east, causing the beaches on the East Coast of the United States to get smaller as those on the West Coast get bigger.

4. When red-hot magma flows out through cracks in the earth's crust under the middle of the ocean, doesn't it immediately harden when it reaches the cold ocean water, just like melted wax or chocolate hardens when poured into cold water?

Yes, as magma reaches the water its surface hardens, forming a crust that cracks as it is continuously pushed up by hot magma below. The ridges that form on the bottom of the ocean, therefore, have a very cracked-looking surface.

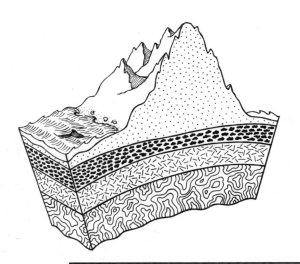

If You Had Been There

I magine that you were alive about two hundred years ago. Your family was thrilled when they heard that President Jefferson had purchased the Louisiana Territory, an area bigger than the entire United States at that time, and they decided to establish a new home in the wilderness. You didn't know what to expect when you left your old home and friends in the city of Philadelphia and traveled westward until you reached the shore of the giant Mississippi River, south of what is now St. Louis. To begin your trek into the new territory, you had to wait for a boat to take you across the river. Finally, in early December 1811, your father found a boatman willing to take you and your whole family across with all your possessions.

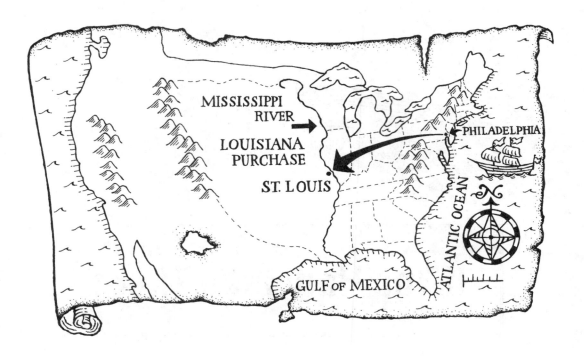

High up on the far shore, you helped your family build a temporary shelter, where you would spend your first winter in the wilderness. While it was still dark on the morning of December 16, your dog became restless and started moaning and baying, waking you out of a sound sleep. You pushed him away to try to get back to sleep, but suddenly the ground began to rumble and shake—and you were scared stiff. The timbers of your shelter creaked and the ground rose and fell as if it were an ocean wave, continuing for what felt like an eternity. Outside, you could hear the trees groan as they were bent by the force of the passing wave. While waiting for the sun to rise, you stayed huddled together with your family, not knowing what to expect next. After dawn another shock struck, and you could see the ground boiling, jets of sandy water shooting up into the air. A crack appeared in the ground and you were afraid you might fall in it, but fortunately it closed rapidly, leaving only a scar on the face of the earth.

As you looked across the river, you saw that the steep bluff on the far side had slid down to the riverbank and that waves were sweeping up and down the river. The boat you had crossed the river in just a few days earlier was washed up on shore and smashed. A sandy island near the middle of the river had disappeared; it had completely sunk below the water's surface.

For close to a month, shocks almost as strong as the first continued. You and your family, who had thought you were starting an exciting new life in a peaceful territory, were instead living a frightening nightmare. You had survived the most powerful earthquake ever to strike the United States.

At this point, you may very well wonder how such an earthquake could have occurred in the Louisiana Territory in the center of the United States, which is in the middle of a tectonic plate. You read in the first chapter that earthquakes take place along the *boundaries* of tectonic plates. What happened?

Even *seismologists*—scientists who study earthquakes—have not been able to answer this question with absolute certainty. But they believe that a deep-rooted crack exists in the middle of the North American plate and that the 1811 earthquake was caused when this fracture shifted.

And why did your dog "feel" the earthquake before anyone else? Animals seem to be sensitive to *precursors*, vibrations and sounds that precede an earthquake and that we ourselves cannot feel or hear. You will be amazed at how sensitive animals are to earthquake precursors when we explore the issue in chapter 7.

And why did the island disappear in the middle of the river? It did so because when sand is filled with water and is shaken by an earthquake it *liquefies,* or flows as if it were a liquid.

Liquefaction

You'll Need

▶ pail

▶ sand (enough to fill the pail)

▶ brick

▶ water

1. Fill a pail with dry sand and set a brick vertically on the level sand surface. If you shake the pail slightly, as if it were hit by an earthquake, the brick may shake but it will not collapse.

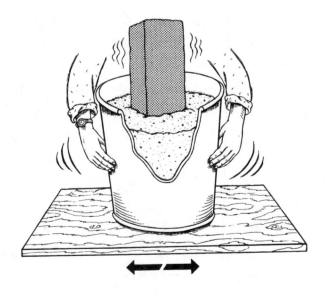

2. Next, add water to the sand-filled pail until it reaches the very level of the sand surface, thus *saturating* the sand with water.

3. Now shake the pail, as you did before you poured in the water. This time, the brick will slowly sink into the sand, tilting or toppling over or even disappearing. The brick behaves like a tall building on mushy soil and shows how the water acts as a *lubricant*, allowing the brick to slide into the sand.

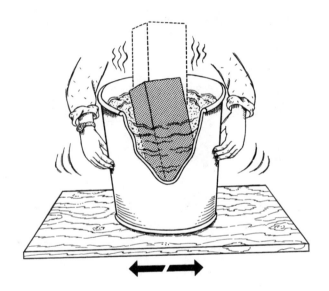

The same phenomenon takes place when a building is set on weak soil and, particularly, on soil near a sandy seashore where it is completely saturated. Liquefaction is a very dangerous phenomenon in earthquake areas.

Questions

1. Our summer home on the California coast is built on the side of a steep hill. Are we safe?

It depends on whether your home is well built and, above all, on the type of soil on which it stands. Loose soil may slide down the hill in a strong earthquake, but rocky soil will not. Clay soil becomes "soapy" under heavy rains, although it is a good soil when dry. If it hasn't been done before, it may be advisable for your parents to have the soil and the foundation under your home checked by an experienced contractor or engineer.

2. We live in Japan in a high-rise apartment building. I am nervous thinking about the possibility that our building could fall down. What could happen?

The Japanese government—and all governments, for that matter—are trying to guard against something terrible happening by making certain that builders follow strict rules to make buildings strong enough to remain standing in an earthquake. Some years ago, during an earthquake in Niigata, Japan, an apartment building built on sand that liquefied tilted almost totally on its side without breaking up so that the occupants could safely reach the ground by walking down the facade. On the other hand, in a more recent, disastrous earthquake in Kobe, Japan, the earth shook so violently that many apartment buildings on soft soil collapsed.

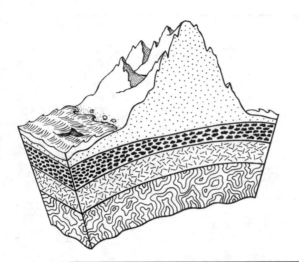

When the Ocean Rolls

I n chapter 1 you learned that the magma of the earth's mantle is very hot. Because the temperature is not the same throughout the mantle, the magma develops *hot rivers* that move in circular motions, rising and falling under the earth's crust.

Convection

You'll Need
► adult helper
► cooking pot
► water
► stove
► rice
► 2 pieces of toasted bread, 50 mm (2 in.) square

1. With the help of a parent or other adult, place a pot of water on the stove and turn on the heat.

2. When the water boils, drop a few grains of rice into the pot.

3. Watch carefully as the water pushes the grains of rice in a circular motion, up the sides of the pot, then away from them near the surface of the water, then down to the bottom in the center of the pot, and finally back up the pot's side. The grains of rice are moved by *convection currents*, just as the hot rivers of magma move around the mantle.

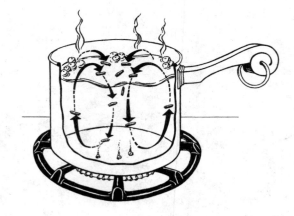

4. Now carefully drop two squares of toasted bread into the water. Notice that the pieces of bread move toward the center of the pot, and that sometimes one piece of bread rubs against the other, while at other times one piece dips under the other.

This experiment demonstrates how tectonic plates are driven by convection currents and move about our planet, causing earthquakes when they bump into each other and opening cracks called *rifts* through which magma flows up.

You have already learned that when the edges of two plates scrape against each other, an earthquake will occur. The edges of most tectonic plates do not lie on land but under the seas, which cover over 70 percent of our planet. When one plate pushes up suddenly against another at the bottom of the sea, the shock also pushes up a mound of water. As the mound settles down, a wave called a *tsunami* (after the Japanese word for "seashore village wave") moves out in all directions on the surface of the ocean, like the waves that radiate from a pebble thrown into a pond.

Generating a Tsunami

You can reproduce this ocean phenomenon the next time you take a bath in the tub.

You'll Need
▶ bathtub

1. Fill a bathtub with water.

2. Once the water surface is level, slowly lower your open hand close to the bottom of the tub.

3. Now move your hand up rapidly a short distance. You have actually "moved up" part of the water at the bottom of the tub, and you should see the surface of the water move in tsunami waves.

You may at one time have made a circular wave appear on the calm waters of a pond by tossing a stone into it, then watched the wave move outward in bigger and bigger circles. What you may not have noticed is that as the circular wave moves outward on the surface of the pond, the water particles of the pond move briefly up and down but remain where they were before you dropped the stone. You can easily check that the water particles stay put by noticing that as the wave goes by, a leaf lying on the pond's surface moves up and down, but does not follow the wave's outward movement (facing page). This happens because a wave is the motion of the water shape but not of the water particles in the direction of the wave.

Tsunamis start as waves at most 1 meter (3 feet) high. Knowing this, you may reasonably feel that tsunamis cannot be too dangerous. In fact, tsunamis are *extremely* dangerous, because these waves are many kilometers long and the enormous energy they receive from the sudden shifting of the sea floor moves them at speeds of up to 600 kilometers (400 miles) per hour. This allows them to cross entire oceans before crashing ashore.

As a tsunami wave travels toward shore, it changes shape as the lower part of the wave is slowed down by the friction between the water and the sea floor, while its top, unrestrained by friction, moves faster and faster and increases in height as the sea floor slopes up. When the wave reaches the shore, a tsunami may be a wall of water 30 meters (100 feet) high.

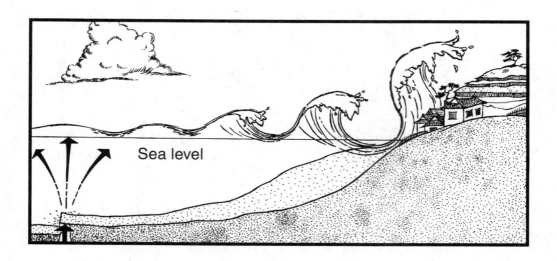

Sea level

When these incredibly powerful waves, these walls of water, finally crash on the shore, they destroy beaches, harbors, houses, and anything else in their path. It is because these waves smash into seaside villages that the Japanese named them "seashore village waves." If they hit a harbor, they may throw the anchored ships onto the land and destroy the docks. When they hit the mouth of a river, they run inland along the river valley, playing havoc with houses, destroying vegetation, and killing people and animals. Then the tsunami rushes back down the valley, carrying into the ocean the ruins of the villages and the bodies of its victims.

Tsunami in a Tub

This experiment should give you a physical feeling for the horror of a real tsunami.

You'll Need

▸ bathtub
▸ 2 plastic tub mats

▶ 6 bricks

▶ many small wooden cubes, about 25 mm (1 in.) on each side

▶ square sheet of plywood, about 300 mm (1 ft.) on each side

1. Fill a bathtub with 100 millimeters (4 inches) of water. To avoid scratches, place a tub mat on the bottom of the tub, near the faucet end.

2. Set two piles of two bricks each on the tub mat, 300 millimeters (1 foot) from the faucet end. Leave a gap of 50 millimeters (2 inches) between the two brick piles.

3. Place the last two-brick pile on the mat about 150 millimeters (6 inches) behind the other two (almost under the faucet).

4. Set another tub mat in front of the bricks to generate friction at the bottom of your "tsunami."

5. Build a number of "buildings" with the wooden cubes on top of the three two-brick piles.

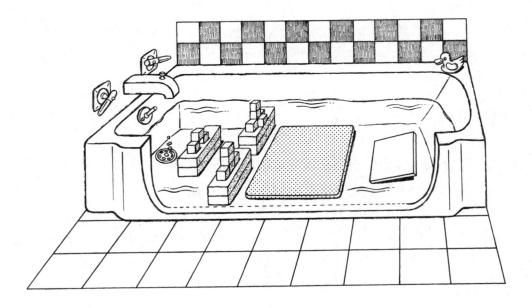

6. Now set the plywood sheet near the sloping end of the tub, slightly inclined toward that end. Push it rapidly forward about 15 centimeters (6 inches), displacing the water in front of it in a "tsunami."

7. Your "tsunami" should rush toward the bricks. Its bottom water will be slowed down by the friction against the tub mat, and the top water will collapse the "buildings" on the first two brick piles. It will then move through the gap between those piles at an even greater speed and destroy the "buildings" in the "valley" beyond.

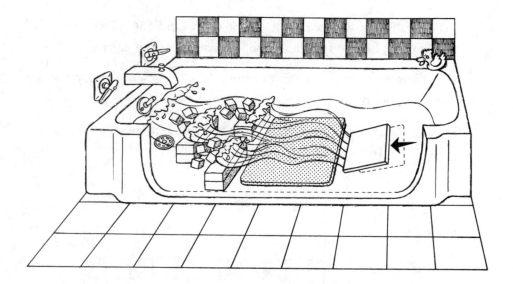

Questions

1. We live on the coast of California. Do we have to worry about being overrun by a tsunami?

Most earthquakes along the California coast are caused by the horizontal slippage between the Pacific and the North American plates. This does not result in a tsunami. However, the West Coast has been struck by tsunamis originating in Alaska and even as far away as Japan.

2. How much time do I have to get away from an arriving tsunami and climb to higher ground?

Because tsunamis travel at airplane speeds, if you see one coming you have only minutes. The governments of both the United States and Japan have tried to give people more time by establishing tsunami warning stations, about 4 kilometers (2.5 miles) out in the ocean, which will detect an arriving tsunami and automatically broadcast a warning. After a recent devastating tsunami in the Indian Ocean, similar warning stations have been established in that part of the world as well.

3. What happens to boats on the ocean as a tsunami passes?

Nothing! In fact, if you were in a boat, you might never even notice the passing wave, because it would very slowly and gently lift and lower the boat. That is because, unlike the short waves at the beach—where you can see many crests approaching—a tsunami wave is very long and you cannot even see from one crest to another.

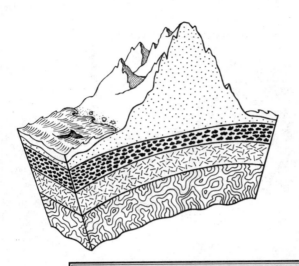

Earthquake Messages

The force of an earthquake comes from *seismic waves* that move through the earth (*seismic* comes from the Greek *seismos*, meaning "earthquake"). The waves originate at the point below the surface of the earth where the tectonic plates move or slip; this point is called the earthquake's *focus*. The focus is considered *shallow* when it is between 0 and 70 kilometers (43 miles) in the crust, and *deep* when it is greater than 300 kilometers (186 miles) deep. The depth of the focus in the crust influences the earthquake's effect: a shallow-focus earthquake will shake you more violently than a deep-focus earthquake of the same strength.

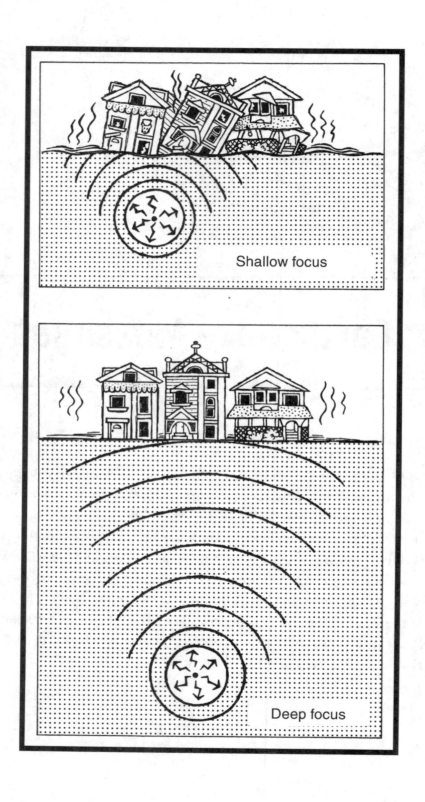

Shallow focus

Deep focus

As they travel out from the focus, seismic waves move the particles of the materials through which they travel, vibrating in a variety of different ways.

Pressure Waves

You'll Need

▶ Slinky (steel or plastic)

▶ table

▶ helper

1. Set the Slinky on a table and grab one end. Ask a friend to grab the other end.

2. Pull and stretch the Slinky to the full length of the table.

3. Move your hand quickly toward your friend, first forward and then back. You will see a wave—a pack of Slinky rings close to each other—move along the Slinky, starting from your end and moving toward your friend, and then back toward you. In other words, the wave shape moves the Slinky rings (the material it crosses) in the same direction as the Slinky.

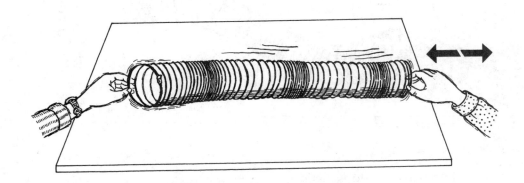

This kind of wave is known as a *pressure wave*. Because the particles of the Slinky vibrate in the same direction as the wave, the pressure wave (sometimes abbreviated *P wave*) is called a *longitudinal wave*.

Shear Waves

You'll Need

► Slinky (steel or plastic)
► table
► helper

1. Stretch a Slinky across a table as you did in the previous experiment.

2. While your friend holds one end of the Slinky steady, wiggle your end to the right and left horizontally.

3. Watch as a pack of Slinky rings moves to the left and right while the wave moves along the length of the Slinky.

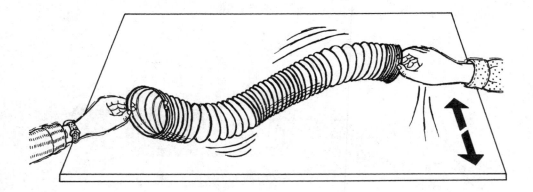

The wave you observed this time is called a *shear wave* (sometimes abbreviated *S wave*) or a *transverse wave*.

The focus of an earthquake emits both pressure and shear waves, both of which are called *body waves* (presumably because they originate in the body of the earth). As with the Slinky, some seismic waves move the particles of the earth at right angles to the direction of the wave, either vertically, like the water surface of a pond into which a pebble has been thrown, or horizontally.

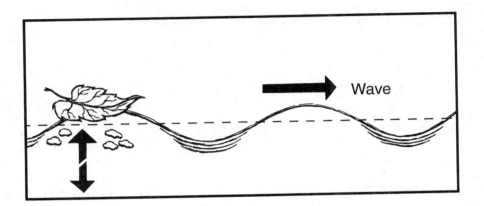

Other waves move the particles back and forth in the direction of the wave motion, like the waves radiating from a hammer blow on rock.

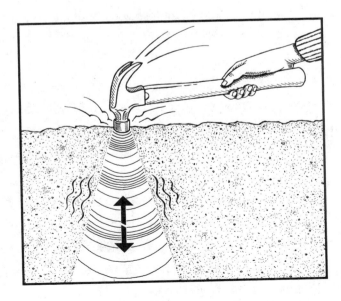

When these two types of body waves reach the earth's surface, they give rise to *surface waves*, which are again of two types that act exactly like pressure and shear waves. Earth scientists have named them *Rayleigh waves* and *Love waves*, after two famous 19th-century British scientists.

The Speed of Waves

You'll Need
- ▶ string
- ▶ door handle

1. Attach one end of a length of string to a door handle and hold the other end in your hand.

2. Move your hand up and down or sideways and watch the shear waves moving along the length of the string.

3. Now hold the line tightly with one hand and pluck the string with your other hand. You will again see shear waves moving along the string.

4. Think about what this experiment tells you about the speed of waves. The tighter you pull the string, the faster the waves will move.

Not all waves travel at the same speed. Pressure waves are the fastest to reach the surface of the earth from the focus. Shear waves travel at about half the speed of P waves, and surface waves travel at about the same speed as shear waves. But all seismic waves travel very fast: the slowest, the surface waves, travel at about 3 kilometers (2 miles) *per second*—about 15 times faster than the speed of our fastest jetliners. The speed of the seismic waves depends on the type of material they cross. They move faster across hard rock and slower across weak soil, just as you can run faster on a hard pavement than through a muddy field.

Wave Reflection

You'll Need

► wall mirror
► handheld mirror

1. Look at yourself in a wall mirror. What you see is a reflection of the light waves that bounce off your body (after all, if it were dark you would not be able to see yourself). In the same way that a ball tossed against a hard surface bounces back, the light waves bounce off the reflective surface of the mirror.

2. Now hold a hand mirror in front of your face while your back faces the wall mirror. As you turn your body, find a position where you can see a reflection of your back, with your face showing in the hand mirror. The same way a ball hitting a wall at an angle will bounce back at an opposite angle, as you turn the light wave of your image bounces off the mirror at an angle opposite to that at which it struck the mirror.

3. Try to explain how the light waves are bouncing around to create the double image you see.

Wave Refraction

You'll Need

▶ drinking straw

▶ clear drinking glass

▶ water

1. Dip a drinking straw in a partially filled glass of water.

2. Observe the glass and the straw from the side. At the level of the top of the water, the straw appears to be bent. What do you think is happening?

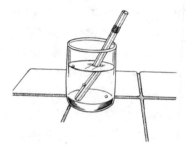

This apparent bending is due to a phenomenon called *refraction*. When the visual waves from the straw pass through the water, they don't bounce off like they would with a mirror, but they do change speed. This change in speed causes them to move in a slightly different direction than the waves that pass through the air, which is why the straw appears bent.

When seismic waves cross from one kind of material to another, they too change direction, in which case we say that they are *refracted* like the straw in the glass of water, or they can be *reflected*, like your image in a mirror.

Shear waves have an additional important property: they cannot travel through liquids and, in particular, through water. That is because water has no *shear strength* (also called *shear resistance*), so the wave behaves as if there were nothing there.

The Strength of Water

You'll Need

► clear drinking glass
► water
► plastic knife

1. Fill a glass with water.

2. Take a plastic knife and plunge it into the water. You note that the water offers no resistance to your action. This is because water has no shear strength.

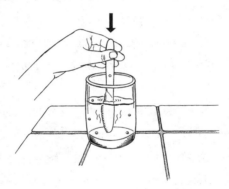

3. Now, move the knife sideways against the flat, broad side of the knife. Notice that it takes some effort to push it back and forth. This is because water does have *compressive strength*.

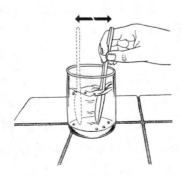

Since S waves cannot move through water, they must travel longer distances through the crust of the earth under the oceans before they are detected by seismographic stations (chapter 5). Scientists can measure the differences in arrival times between P and S waves to help pin down the location of the focus of an earthquake. The difference in speed between P and S waves is also useful in determining the quake's focus, while the refraction and reflection of the waves tell us much about the nature of the soils they cross.

Questions

1. The interior of the earth, the mantle, is very hot. In fact, it is hot enough to melt rock. I just read that S waves cannot travel through a liquid, yet S waves travel through the mantle. How does this happen?

The soupy rock of the mantle is under tremendous pressure from the weight of the crust above it and, as a result, its melting temperature is much greater than it would be on the surface of the earth, just as the temperature of steam in a kitchen pressure cooker is much greater than it would be in the open air. Because it is under such high pressure, and thus has a high melting temperature, the mantle therefore feels like a solid to S waves.

2. Are the waves coming from the focus similar to those I hear when a bell is struck?

Yes. In fact, a 17th-century Belgian chemist, J. B. van Helmont, was the first to suggest that the vibrations felt in an earthquake originated when an avenging angel struck a huge celestial bell. Of course, we now know that the cause is not an avenging angel, but the idea anticipated the scientific explanation of waves coming from an earthquake focus.

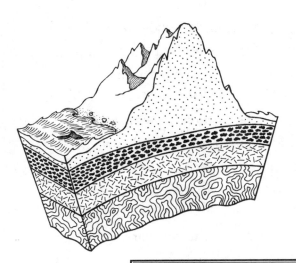

How Strong Was It?

At some time you have probably heard on television and radio or from your parents an announcement like "Yesterday at 4:00 A.M. an earthquake measuring 4 on the Richter scale was felt in Long Beach, California. No deaths have been reported and only minor damage to buildings has occurred." Or "Today at 4:30 P.M. an earthquake of Richter magnitude 7 hit San Francisco, killing one hundred people and causing millions of dollars worth of damage." You may gather from such announcements that the Richter scale 4 earthquake in Long Beach was a weak earthquake, but the Richter scale 7 earthquake in San Francisco was devastatingly strong. What is the meaning of the numbers on the Richter scale?

Almost three hundred years ago seismologists started recording the impact earthquakes had on people and buildings. These

45

records were not well organized, so in the early 1900s the Italian seismologist Giuseppe Mercalli suggested a standard list based on the amount of damage done to buildings and on the reaction of people to earthquakes. This is now called the *Modified Mercalli scale*, which defines 12 levels of damage. But the opinions of witnesses are very personal and, hence, can be widely different. To be thrown out of bed by an earthquake may be a terrible experience for an American to whom this has happened for the first time, but it may be nothing extraordinary to a Japanese person who has had a number of such experiences. A better way of estimating an earthquake's strength had to be found.

And this is what the American seismologist Charles Richter did in 1935 by proposing to estimate the strength of earthquakes by scientifically measuring both the motions of the earth's crust during an earthquake and the energy of the earthquake shock.

You may wonder how Richter was able to measure the earth's crust motions and the energy of an earthquake. He did it by means of a measuring instrument called a *seismograph*.

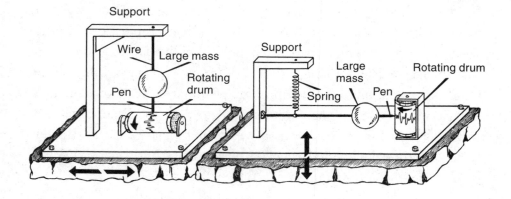

But before you learn what a seismograph is, you should study an instrument first used by Chinese scientists almost two thousand years ago that creates a "picture" of the earth's motions. It is called a *seismometer*. To measure the motions of an earthquake, you need three seismometers: two of the same type to measure the horizontal motion of the earth's surface, both front and back and left and right, and another type to measure the vertical motion.

Build a Seismometer

Here's how to build the first type of seismometer, which measures the horizontal motions of the earth's surface.

You'll Need
- large cereal box
- scissors
- strip of paper about 50 mm (2 in.) wide by 600 mm (2 ft.) long
- pencil
- plastic or cardboard cup with cover
- sand
- piece of string
- small stick (the size of a match)
- sheet of cardboard about the size of a cereal box

1. Cut a large rectangle out of both large sides of a cereal box, leaving edges 25 millimeters (1 inch) wide.

2. Cut in the middle of the bottom edges two narrow horizontal slots a little more than 50 millimeters (2 inches) wide, and slide through the paper strip you have prepared.

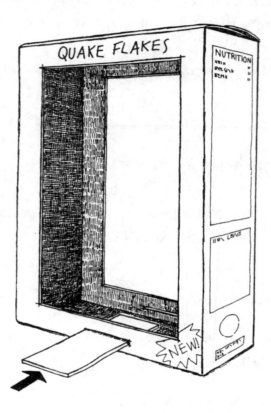

3. Pierce a hole through the center of the top cover of a plastic or cardboard cup and another at the bottom of the cup. Push a pencil, point down, through the two holes. Remove the cover and fill the cup with sand so that the pencil stands vertical.

4. Thread the string through two holes near the top of opposite sides of the cup. Hang the cup from the center of the top of the cereal box by tying the string around a small stick at the center of the box top, as shown. Replace the cover of the cup.

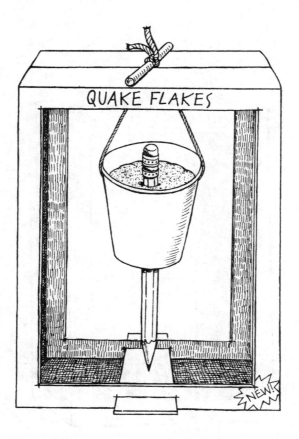

5. Adjust the length of the string so that the tip of the pencil touches the strip of paper you have threaded through the bottom cuts in the box.

6. Glue the bottom of the cereal box to the large sheet of cardboard. Let the glue dry.

7. Now try it out! Notice that if you move the cardboard sheet back and forth, the weighted pencil stays put and makes a mark on the paper strip you have passed through the cardboard base.

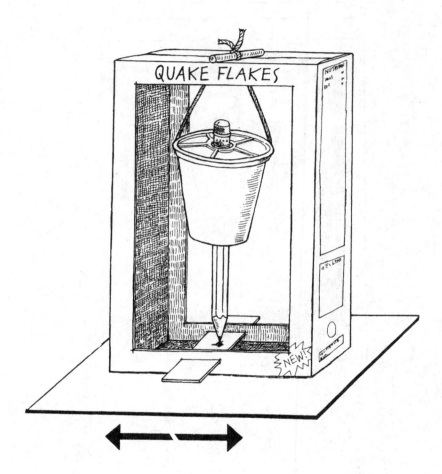

QUAKE FLAKES

How does a seismometer work? It takes advantage of a property called *inertia*, which is common to anything with weight—that is, to any mass. Inertia shows that the basic property of a mass is to be "lazy." If an object is moving, it will refuse to move faster or slower unless pushed or pulled by a force. If it is at rest, it will stay put unless pulled or pushed by a force. A car moving on a flat road will keep on moving unless slowed by the application of a brake force, and it will move faster only when pushed by higher engine speeds. You may have observed that a spinning top, if pushed, does not fall but comes right back to a vertical position. This is because of its *rotational inertia*.

What you have built by hanging a weight (in this case, the sand-filled cup) from a string is a fascinating device called a *pendulum*.

A Pendulum

You can easily build a pendulum with nothing more than a weight and a string.

You'll Need
- ▶ small weight (stone or heavy steel bolt)
- ▶ string
- ▶ clock or watch with second hand
- ▶ helper
- ▶ ruler

1. Hang a small weight from a string and hold the upper end of the string in one hand.

2. Push the weight once with your other hand so that it swings back and forth.

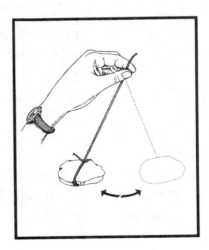

3. While doing this, look at the second hand of a clock or watch and see how long it takes for the weight to move from the extreme left to the extreme right and back again.

(It might be easier to see how long it takes to complete 10 swings, then divide the time by 10.) This interval of time is called the *period* of the pendulum.

4. Lengthen the string and repeat the experiment. You should notice that the period becomes longer.

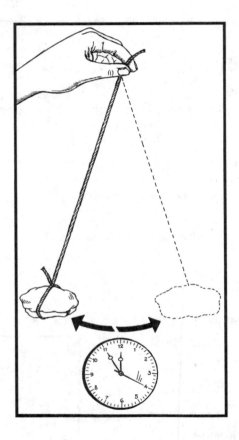

5. Now shorten the string and repeat the experiment. The period will become shorter.

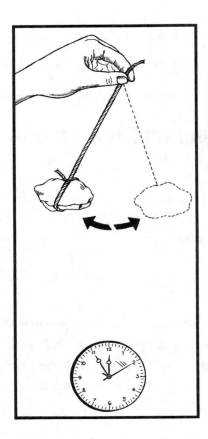

6. Now have a friend hold a ruler horizontally at the level of the hanging weight and repeat the swinging experiment. Ask your friend to tell you the measurement indicated on the ruler as the pendulum swings to the extreme left and when it swings to the extreme right. By subtracting the smaller from the larger number, you have measured the *amplitude* of the movement.

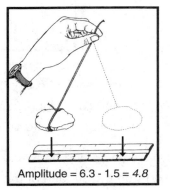

Amplitude = 6.3 - 1.5 = *4.8*

You will find that both period and amplitude are important properties that measure how fast and how strong an earthquake is.

Another Pendulum Experiment

You'll Need
► pendulum (from previous experiment)
► pencil
► paper
► tape

1. For this experiment, use the pendulum you built in the previous experiment. First, hold the pendulum still and move your hand, quickly but slightly, right and left. The inertia of the weight will prevent it from moving, and it will stay almost put.

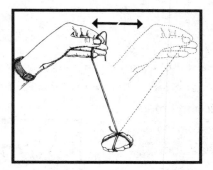

2. Now hold a pencil horizontally in your hand together with the top of the pendulum string. Tape a sheet of paper to a wall so that it is high enough to write on while holding the pendulum.

3. Shake your hand back and forth as if it were connected to a point on the surface of the earth that is being moved by an earthquake.

4. Start your "earthquake" by moving your hand fast enough to prevent the weight from moving; touch the pencil to the top of the
paper and slowly move your hand downward. The pencil will
draw a graph of your hand's motion that is similar to a graph
measuring the movement of the earth's crust due to an earthquake. Since the weight stays put while your hand, representing
the earthquake, moves, you have created a simple instrument
that models the earth's seismic motion with respect to a fixed
point!

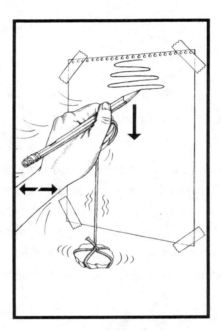

So far your experiments have simulated *how much* the earth
moves during an earthquake, but scientists also like to know how
fast it moves and over what length of time. When you measured the
period of the pendulum, you used a clock or watch to tell you how
long the motion took. By adding the measure of time, you can now
convert your seismometer into a seismograph.

The Seismograph

You'll Need

► seismometer (from experiment on p. 47)
► clock or watch with second hand
► 2 pencils
► large cereal box
► scissors
► strip of paper about 50 mm (2 in.) wide by 600 mm (2 ft.) long
► plastic or cardboard cup with cover
► sand
► pencil
► 3 rubber bands
► small stick (the size of a match)

1. Shake the "earth" cardboard base of your seismometer back and forth with one hand in the direction parallel to the large sides of the box, while at the same time slowly but steadily sliding the paper strip with your other hand. The pencil draws a *seismogram* of the "earthquake" because while you shake the box, the pencil in the cup stays put due to the inertia of the sand in the cup.

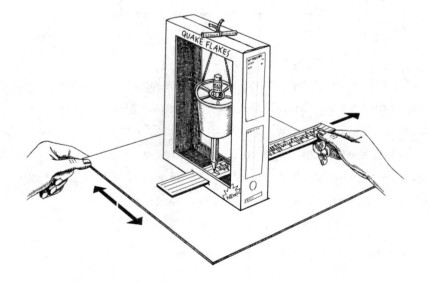

2. Measure with a watch the time you have shaken your "earth-quake." Draw a line down the paper strip and mark seconds by dividing the length of the graph by the duration of the "earth-quake." You have thus obtained the graph of your earthquake motions against time—a working seismograph.

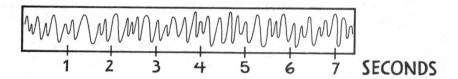

1   2   3   4   5   6   7   **SECONDS**

3. After you learn to shake the box skillfully, you may try to imitate the graph below, which represents the horizontal seismogram of a real earthquake. (**NOTE:** Unless you have four hands, you may need to ask a friend to be your timekeeper.)

4. Now build a second kind of seis-mograph, which measures the *vertical* movements of the earth due to an earthquake. Cut a large rectangle from both large sides of another cereal box and cut small vertical slits for the strip of paper near the edge of two opposite narrow vertical sides of the box, right next to the cut vertical large sides of the box. Slide through the paper strip.

5. Make two holes in opposite sides of another cup, near its top. Thread a pencil horizontally through both holes, fill the cup with sand, and cover the top.

6. Hang the cup from the center of the top of the box with two rubber bands tied at the top to a stick, and at the bottom to the two projecting ends of the pencil.

7. Adjust the pencil so that it touches the horizontally sliding paper strip.

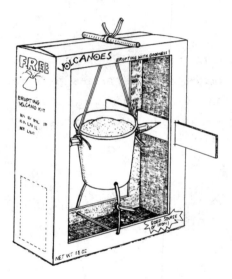

8. Stabilize the cup by tying a cut-open rubber band from the bottom of the cup to the bottom of the frame.

9. To measure the vertical motions of your "earthquake," shake the cereal box up and down with one hand, while sliding the paper strip toward you horizontally with your other hand. The pencil in the box will stay put because of the inertia of the sand-filled cup and will graph the motions while you shake the box up and down.

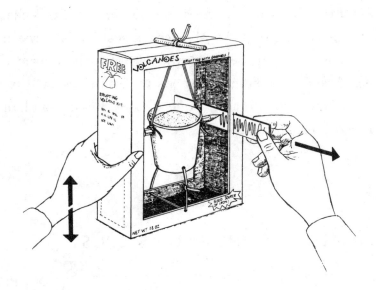

10. Graph the seismogram of the vertical motion versus time as you
    did with the seismogram for the horizontal motion. (Measure the
    time it takes to move the strip of paper and mark it on the strip.)

Using the measurements from a seismograph, Dr. Richter
developed a scale to define the magnitude of an earthquake. In
order to grasp the meaning of the numbers of the Richter scale, you
must become acquainted with its two main features. First, the
Richter magnitude scale assigns a value of 1 to a barely felt earthquake and goes up to a value of about 9 for the strongest earthquake. So far, the strongest quake ever registered had a value of
about 9, but seismologists do not believe that an earthquake much
stronger than 9 has a chance of ever occurring.

Second, an increase of 1 in the numbers of the Richter scale of
ground motion means an increase of 10 in the motions of the
earth's crust. (Mathematicians call such scales *logarithmic scales*
with base 10.) In the hypothetical examples of the Long Beach and

the San Francisco earthquakes at the beginning of this chapter, the San Francisco earthquake of Richter scale 7 is three numbers higher than the Long Beach earthquake of Richter scale 4. Hence, the San Francisco earthquake shook the earth's crust 10 x 10 x 10, or 1,000 times more, than the one at Long Beach—and, of course, did much greater damage.

MOVEMENT OF THE EARTH'S CRUST

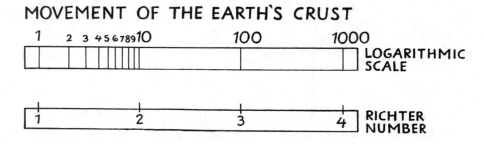

Seismographic stations have now been established all over the world to measure the strength of earthquakes. These stations can also be used to pinpoint the location of an earthquake—since, remember, the two main types of seismic waves travel at different speeds. By measuring the difference in the arrival times of P and S waves, the distance from the focus of the earthquake to the seismographic station can be calculated. By using the reports of the arrival time of the P and S waves from three different seismographic stations, the exact location of the earthquake can be pinpointed.

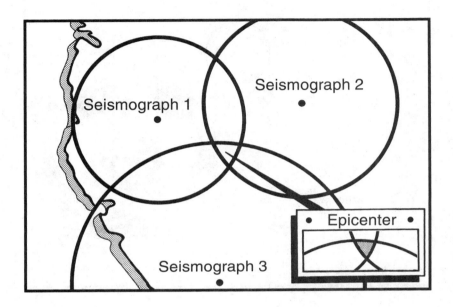

Questions

1. Is there a way to visualize what the Richter scale really means?

Think of the magnitude scale being represented by the volume of a series of balls. If you start with a marble to represent a magnitude 1 quake, a magnitude 3 quake would be a golf ball, a magnitude 4 would be a baseball and a magnitude 5 would be a soccer ball.

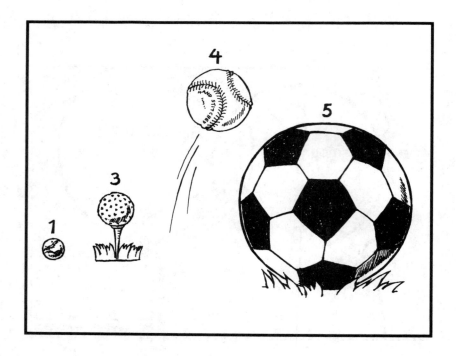

2. How many earthquakes occur every year?

There are about a million earthquakes on the planet every year, most of which are too weak to be felt. About 150,000 are strong enough for people to feel them. However, there are only about 19 strong enough to cause serious damage, and many of these occur in uninhabited areas or under the oceans.

3. I heard that a very strong earthquake struck Alaska in the last century. How bad was it?

In 1964 a magnitude 8.4 quake, centered in Prince William Sound, caused tremendous damage to Anchorage, Alaska. It was the strongest quake to hit the North American continent in over one hundred years, and since its focus was under the sea, it spawned a major tsunami that overran beaches and harbors as far away as Hawaii and California. In fact, the quake was so powerful that even Cuba, more than 6,400 kilometers (4,000 miles) away, shook slightly.

3. I was visiting Shanghai, China, in March 2008 when the building I was in began to shake. I thought that Shanghai was not in an active seismic zone. What happened?

Almost 1,500 kilometers (900 miles) away in Sichuan Province there was a major earthquake of magnitude 7.9. It was so powerful that it was felt in Bankok, Thailand, more than 2,000 kilometers (1,200 miles) away. The fact that you felt the shock even though you were so far from the focus of the quake is an indication of its strength. Together with numerous strong aftershocks, this quake caused extensive damage and loss of life.

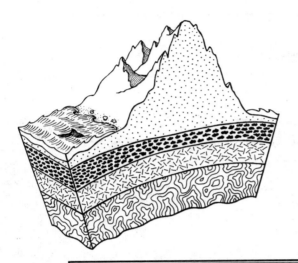

From Myth to Science

In the time it takes you to read this sentence, somewhere on earth there will be an earthquake. You will not be aware of it because it may well have struck somewhere under an ocean or hit some uninhabited part of the world, or, more likely, it was too weak to be felt by humans. Only fish in the oceans, animals on land, and maybe even the plants were witnesses to the quake. If it had been a strong one, which happens only at most six times a year, it would have been reported in the news and you might have seen its impact on television. A super earthquake, of magnitude above 8 on the Richter scale, happens about once a year, and you would certainly have heard of it—because even if its origin was under the ocean or in some uninhabited place, it would have been felt in a town or city occupied by people.

The Shaking Experiment

You'll Need

- ▶ 2 rolling pins (the kind used to make pie crusts)
- ▶ board, same width as the length of the rolling pins and about 1 m (3 ft.) long
- ▶ helper
- ▶ clock or watch with second hand

1. Place the rolling pins on the floor and put the board on top of them so that the ends of the board overhang the pins by about the width of a hand.

2. Carefully stand on the board with your feet slightly apart for stability.

3. Have your friend grasp one end of the board and pull it very slowly no more than 50 millimeters (2 inches), and push it back equally slowly to the starting point. Notice that if the board is pulled and pushed very, very slowly, you do not feel the movement.

4. Have your friend look at a watch or clock and count the number of times in a minute he or she pushes and then pulls the board, thus concluding one complete movement, called a *cycle*. That number is the frequency in cycles per minute of the movement of the board.

5. Now have your friend move the board at a faster speed and record the frequency. Keep repeating the experiment at increasing speeds until you first sense the movement by feeling unsteady, then note the frequency at which this occurs. *Be careful*, because if your friend pushes and pulls the board too fast, you will fall off—as you would fall down in a very shaky earthquake.

Perhaps because people are less sensitive to earthquake vibrations, while animals respond to even the slightest shaking, for centuries people all over the world believed that animals were responsible for earthquakes.

In the mythical tales of the inhabitants of southern Russia, a giant bull living under the earth's surface was said to be the cause of earthquakes. In southern Chile an old legend attributed earthquakes to the fighting between two snakes, one who dug holes to store water in the earth and another who filled the holes with stones to prevent the first from storing the water. In ancient China the winged dragon-snake Lung shook the earth on its horns, and in India an elephant-god was the cause of earthquakes.

A frog did it in Central Asia, and in Japan it was caused by the thrashing of Namazu, a giant catfish. On the Kamchatka peninsula of northern Asia, an underground dog was responsible for the earth's tremors, and in Mexico a jaguar. The Bull of Knossos shook the Greek island of Crete, and a goddess shook ancient Babylon, today's Iraq. The members of certain Native American nations believed that the earth was supported by a giant tortoise and that whenever the tortoise took a step, the earth trembled.

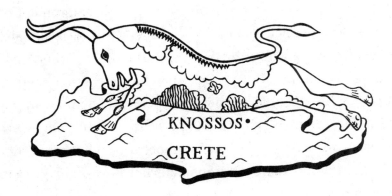

Modern science has at long last explained that earthquakes are due to the motions of the tectonic plates, not to mythical animals. But so far seismologists have only been able to answer the first of the two questions concerning us most: they can predict *where* the next earthquake will hit, but *when* an earthquake will hit a specific area is a question that still baffles them.

Seismologists believe that the location of all future earthquakes will eventually become predictable, thanks to a worldwide network of seismographic stations capable of sensing the weakest precursor shocks, the small vibrations resulting from the realignment of the tectonic plates just before a major slippage. (It is these signals that some believe are felt by animals.) Yet at the present time, the best seismologists can do is to predict the chance that an earthquake will occur within a time period of 30 years. They may announce, for example, that there is a 90 percent chance that a strong earthquake, maybe "the Big One," will occur in Southern California within the next 30 years, an important but not totally reassuring piece of information for the citizens of Los Angeles.

Making Predictions

Suppose you were an earthquake scientist and you had made a list of earthquakes and the dates of their occurrence. As you look at the list, you notice that the city of Parkfield, California, seems to have had a large number of moderate earthquakes (of magnitude 6). You write down the dates of all the Parkfield quakes that have been reported and compute the number of years between each quake:

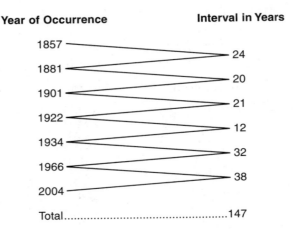

Year of Occurrence

	Interval in Years
1857	24
1881	20
1901	21
1922	12
1934	32
1966	38
2004	
Total...147	

When will the next quake likely occur?

1. Divide the total number of interval years, 147, by the number of intervals, 6, to obtain an average interval of 24.5 years, or approximately 25 years.

2. To make a prediction based on the average interval, add the average to the last occurrence (2004 + 25). You predict that the next earthquake in Parkfield will occur in 2029. But is that the best you can do?

3. Since there was as little as 12 years and as much as 38 years between earthquakes, you could modify your prediction to reflect the range of intervals: it is probable that there will be an earthquake sometime between 2016 (2004 + 12) and 2042 (2004 + 38) in Parkfield.

Guessing the arrival time of future earthquakes by studying the record of past earthquakes is called *extrapolation*. Whenever the *faults* (the cracks produced in the earth's crust by the tectonic plate motions) reach the surface of the earth, seismologists can "read," by looking at the side of the crack, when the plates moved and how much they moved due to earthquakes that occurred from prehistoric times until today. This has been done along one of the longest *superficial faults* (one that left a trace on the earth's surface), the approximately 1,200-kilometer-long (750-mile-long) San Andreas Fault near the California coast.

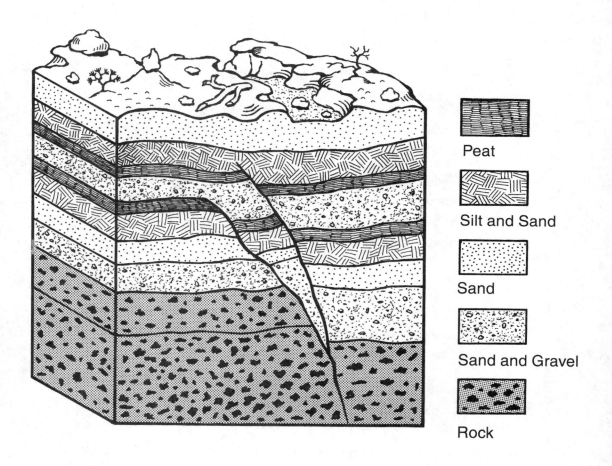

Peat

Silt and Sand

Sand

Sand and Gravel

Rock

On the basis of records dating back about two hundred years, a *seismic risk map* of the United States is published by the U.S. Geological Survey in which five types of regions labeled 0 to 4 identify the strength of the earthquakes to be expected. The 0 areas are those that have never suffered earthquakes—that is, the safest. Areas that have experienced earthquakes of increasing strength are labeled 1 to 4.

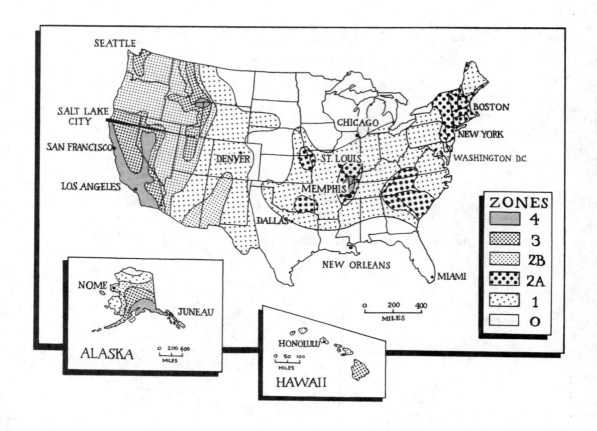

Mapping the Risk

You'll Need

► U.S. Geological Survey risk map (see above)

1. Using the risk map, first locate the state in which you live and then try to pinpoint your hometown. Which zone do you live in? If, for instance, you live in Memphis, you are in zone 3, which carries a serious risk of earthquakes. On the other hand, if you live in New Orleans, you need not be concerned about earthquakes, because you are in zone 0.

2. Study the map and locate the homes of your friends and family to determine their earthquake risk.

Another recent approach to earthquake warning, adopted first in China and now in Japan and the United States as well, consists of gathering information about the minor phenomena that often precede an earthquake. Besides the weak precursor shocks you already learned about, changes of water levels in lakes and wells, temperature changes in the depth of the crust, and even changes in the speed of P and S waves (see chapter 4) may help predict an earthquake. With the help of sensitive instruments capable of measuring these minor changes, seismologists may be able to forecast an earthquake quite accurately. They already did so in 1973 in the Adirondack Mountains of New York State, where they measured the small changes in the speed of the precursor P and S waves and were only one day off in predicting a quake's arrival time.

Later in the book, you will learn what precautions you can take to prevent injury if an earthquake is predicted in your area.

Questions

1. Are there maps that identify the risk of earthquakes in countries other than the United States?

Every country has its own maps and often uses different numbers to represent the intensity of earthquakes. Japan, for instance, has a magnitude scale that goes from 0 to 7, compared to the Richter scale that goes from 0 to 9.

2. I live in Missouri, and our teachers make us drill against earthquakes, but we haven't had any since I

started school six years ago. What's the purpose of these drills?

Earthquakes hit when you least expect them. You should take these drills very seriously—they may save your life. Since you are reading this book, you should have learned how dangerous earthquakes can be and that your region suffered one of the strongest earthquakes ever felt in the United States (see chapter 2). You should participate in the drills and even do better than that: you should become a leader in earthquake prevention for your school and your family. If you do, you have nothing to lose and a lot to gain.

3. I live in California and hear that a strong earthquake is due here sometime. I believe they call it "the Big One." When is the Big One supposed to get here?

At this time, seismologists predict that an earthquake of Richter magnitude 8 or above has a 90 percent chance of occurring within 20 years, most probably along the southern San Andreas Fault, in the area of Los Angeles. Nobody knows exactly when it will hit, but everybody should get ready for its arrival right now (see chapter 8 for some suggestions).

4. I don't understand how you can "read" when an earthquake occurred in the past by looking at the side of a crack. Can you explain it?

Soils have been deposited in layers on the surface of the earth over millions of years, either through flows of lava or decomposition of earlier rocks. These layers would look perfectly uniform, like those of a many-layered cake, except that they are distorted by natural disturbances such as floods, erosion, or the mountain-building caused by the pushing together of tectonic plates or by earthquakes. That explains why a cut through the earth looks so jumbled. To determine the date when particular events happened, you have to develop a time scale—by knowing, for instance, when a particular earthquake occurred or when a tree was buried (you may have learned that the age of trees can be determined by counting their rings).

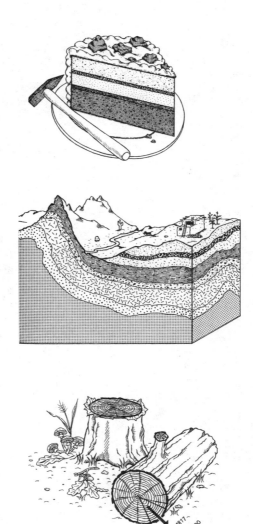

5. I live in Japan and wondered how many quakes I can expect to experience in my life?

Since Japan is in an active seismic zone, you can expect to experience hundreds or maybe even thousands. Fortunately, most are too weak to be felt and cause damage.

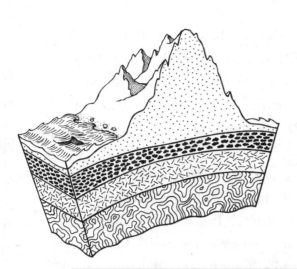

7

Can Animals Predict Earthquakes?

On the night of February 4, 1983, Awilda Salas of Long Beach, California, was sleeping deeply. She was suddenly awakened by the loud chirping of birds in her garden. She could not go back to sleep because the birds kept chirping wildly, but when she eventually did, it was only to be awakened an hour later by an earthquake described in the morning paper the next day as having a Richter magnitude of 5.7 with its epicenter in San Diego. (The *epicenter* is a point on the surface of the earth directly above the focus where the earthquake originated.)

Awilda had never before been awakened in the middle of the night by birds or earthquakes. She firmly believes that on that troubled night the birds had somehow sensed the oncoming earthquake at least one hour before it arrived.

Since time immemorial, people all over the world have believed that animals are sensitive to precursor signals so faint that they cannot be detected even by our best instruments. Two thousand years ago Chinese historians reported strange animal behavior prior to earthquakes, and the Greeks mentioned similar occurrences in 373 B.C.

Not all seismologists believe in the predictive capacity of animals. Yet a German scientist, Dr. Helmut Tributsch, intrigued by the stories he heard from the peasants of the Italian region of Friuli after a devastating earthquake damaged or destroyed a hundred thousand houses (including his family home), has dedicated years of research to the question of animal sensitivity to earthquakes. Among the many examples he mentions in his book *When the Snakes Awake* (MIT Press, 1984), the following are typical:

- A number of witnesses assert that cattle, some of the most placid animals in the world, sense the arrival of earthquakes, and have been known to break out of their corrals and stampede.

- Flocks of birds have been reported flying in circles for hours and then suddenly flying away just before the arrival of an earthquake.

- Mosquitoes and flies have suddenly disappeared from a neighborhood just before an earthquake.

- According to reliable witnesses, a few hours before an earthquake devastated an Asian village, cats ran out of every house.

- Before the arrival of an earthquake along the southern coast of Hokkaido, one of the main islands of Japan, thousands of fish jumped into the air, many landing on beaches and dying.

Unlike the myths described in chapter 6, which blamed animals for *causing* earthquakes, these reports simply attribute to animals a higher sensitivity to precursors. At present, scientific explanations of these reports are not available, nor do we have proof that animals truly can predict earthquakes.

But if dogs can follow the smell of a human being, if birds and even butterflies can fly thousands of miles every year from their winter quarters to the same summer quarters, and if salmon can swim the oceans for months and years and return, thanks to their exceptional sense of smell, to die at the source of the river of their birth, isn't it possible for animals to be particularly sensitive to faint earthquake phenomena?

Question

1. Why don't adults believe that animals can predict earthquakes?

There is a story told by a reporter who was walking past a stable a few hours before the devastating 1906 San Francisco earthquake. He observed the horses crashing around in their stalls and banging their hooves against the doors trying to get out. He thought that the horses were simply agitated—he did not understand that some horrendous event was about to take place. Of course, we now know that this happened just before the earthquake, but we can't blame him for not understanding the horses' agitation because humans usually don't understand what animals are trying to communicate to us in their own way.

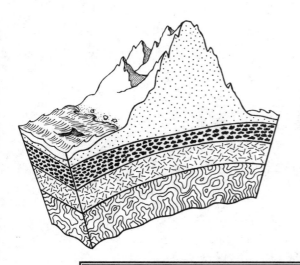

8

Should We Fight or Fool the Quakes?

Modern buildings are very much like human bodies. They are kept up by the structure, which acts just as the bones of our skeletons do. They are enclosed by their facades, which are like our skin. Their windows are like our eyes, and they breathe through their air-conditioning systems, which act like our lungs. They have an electronic computer system that monitors and controls their mechanical and electrical operations just as we have a brain in our head controlling our functions. They are built, live a useful life, and eventually die, just as we are born, live, and die. And just like some of us are hurt in accidents, our buildings are sometimes damaged or destroyed.

Finally, just as doctors take care of our health and try to make sure we live longer and better lives, structural engineers design the structures of our buildings to stand up for many, many years, and repair them when they become weak due to age or misuse. Engineers must make sure that the structure of a building will support its own weight, the so-called *dead load* caused by the pull of gravity. In addition, the weight of people, furniture, and all the other movable elements in the building, the so-called *live load*, has to be supported. The engineer must also make sure that the structure will resist the impact of the wind, which may push and pull the building, or even twist it during a storm or hurricane. And in the seismic areas of the world, structural engineers have an additional difficult job: they must fight earthquakes.

In the past, engineers were unable to prevent earthquakes from damaging or destroying buildings, but they are now beginning to win "the battle of the earthquakes." Today, their work often saves both buildings and lives. In this chapter, we will look at the ways in which we can protect our buildings from most quakes by giving them the needed structural strength and flexibility.

Buildings come in many shapes—to serve as apartment buildings, office high-rises, schools, theaters, sports arenas, churches, jails—and are built with many different materials—steel, reinforced concrete, wood, stone, bricks, or adobe (straw-reinforced mud). All these materials react to the forces acting on them (including weight, wind, and earthquakes) in only two ways: they can either be *pulled* or be *pushed*.

A Push-Pull Demonstration

You'll Need

▶ sponge (thick foam rubber)

▶ scissors

1. From a thick foam rubber sponge, cut a strip about 150 milli-meters (6 inches) long and 50 millimeters (2 inches) wide.

2. Grab the ends of the strip and pull them gently. Notice that as the strip stretches—that is, gets longer—its width decreases as if it had been squeezed.

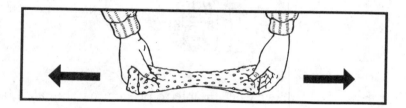

3. Now place the strip of sponge on its side on a table and push down on it. Notice that it gets shorter and at the same time its sides bulge out.

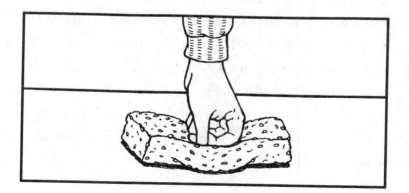

You have just witnessed the two principal actions that a structure experiences, pulling and pushing, or in engineering lingo, *tension* and *compression*. You have also discovered that in the process of being tensed or compressed, the material either squeezes in or bulges out without the volume of the material changing. Of course, building materials are much stiffer than a sponge, so the lengthening and shortening is very, very small and not visible to the naked eye. For example, the cables holding a suspension bridge are in tension and the columns holding up a building are in compression due to the forces acting on them, but you can't see the stretching or shortening taking place.

The job of the structural engineer is to make sure that under the tension and compression forces of the strongest earthquake expected in a seismic area, the materials used for the structure of the buildings in that area will not collapse. To try to achieve this result, all that the engineer must do is satisfy some basic principles.

First, the engineer should avoid making the structure too stiff in the hope of making it strong. A good earthquake-resistant structure should be flexible, a property engineers call *elasticity*. If you have ever seen a strong wind blow on trees, you know that a stiff old oak may suddenly be snapped to the ground by a strong wind gust, while a young sapling bends under the gust's pressure but straightens up again when the wind gust is gone. The oak breaks because it is stiff, while the sapling stands up because it is elastic.

The second and perhaps most important structural principle requires that the building materials will deform permanently instead of breaking, a property known as *ductility*. (It is different from elasticity because it assumes that the materials will not return to their original position, unlike the sapling in the example above.)

A Bending Demonstration

You'll Need

► chalk

► paper clip

1. Take a piece of chalk and try to bend it. It will snap before you can bend it.

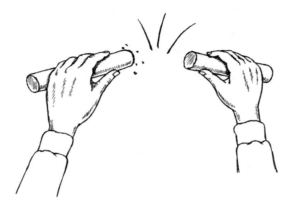

2. Now take a paper clip and bend it back and forth. It will bend a number of times before it breaks. We say that the paper clip is *ductile* and the chalk is *brittle* (it behaves like glass that shatters when hit—or like the old oak branch that snaps suddenly).

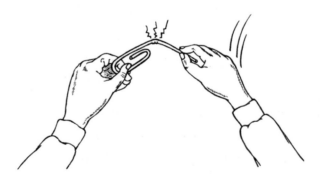

You may have noticed that you worked harder to break the paper clip than the chalk, which means you used more energy breaking the paper clip. In the same way, steel absorbs quite a bit of an earthquake's energy before breaking, while concrete breaks without absorbing much earthquake energy.

In *reinforced concrete,* steel reinforcing bars are added to concrete (which is a brittle material) to improve its ductility. If you visit a construction site, this is one reason that you will see many such steel bars set into the columns and beams of a concrete building, especially in a seismic area.

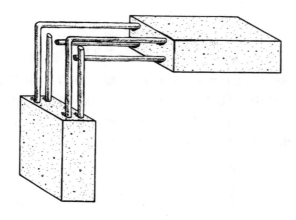

There are, of course, other things that should or should not be done to make our buildings safe from the damaging blows of an earthquake. A building should not be built on weak, mushy soil or on soil permeated with water. During a quake, such soils suffer from liquefaction; they develop high friction, slow the speed of the surface waves (see p. 40), and make the buildings bend back and forth much more than when the speedier pressure waves move through rocky soils. Finally, a structure should not be built on the side of a hill unless it has been carefully checked by an engineer to avoid it being founded on weak soils and possibly tumbling down the hill in an earthquake, as happened in Alaska in 1964.

The importance of these structural principles was shown by the differing behavior of buildings in San Francisco during the Loma Prieta earthquake of 1992. Despite its high 7.1 Richter magnitude, this earthquake did not damage a single skyscraper, because they had all been designed in accordance with the most recent requirements of the building codes, the structural laws established by the building authorities that include the principles for safe structures. According to local witnesses, the skyscrapers swayed *elastically*, like trees in a strong wind, but were not damaged by the earthquake. Unfortunately, older *masonry* buildings (bricks joined with cement mortar), which are more rigid, cracked or crumbled from the force of the quake. In the Marina District, the buildings that stood on *fill* (soil deposited by humans in shallow water outside the original shoreline) were devastated by liquefaction.

In the early 20th century, a totally different approach to earthquake resistance was suggested by people who had an understanding of how the property of inertia could help generate earthquake resistance in a building. They suggested that rather than fighting the earthquakes, it might be easier to "fool" them. They suggested cutting away, or *isolating*, the building from the earth and letting it "float" while the earth moved under it. Inertia would prevent the building from moving and the building would not "feel" the earthquake. (Sounds great but a bit crazy, doesn't it?)

Isolation

In 1909 a British medical doctor made an ingenious suggestion. "Why not put a layer of lubricating talcum powder between a building and its foundation so that the earth may freely slide *under* the building when an earthquake hits while the building stays put due to its inertia?"

You'll Need
▶ talcum (baby) powder
▶ cardboard
▶ empty cereal box
▶ sand or pebbles

1. Sprinkle a layer of talcum powder on a sheet of cardboard.

2. Fill a cereal box with sand or pebbles to make it heavy and, hence, give it inertia.

3. Place the box on the talcum powder–covered cardboard.

4. Shake the cardboard right and left. The cereal box should slide on it and almost stay put.

If the cereal box represents your building and the cardboard the earth's crust, notice that your "building" will move much less than the "earth" and therefore "feel" the earthquake much less. Yet . . . it does not return exactly to its original place, something a real building should always do.

A more ingenious idea was recently proposed. Why not put the building on springs or on rubber pads?

Building on Pads

You'll Need
▶ sponge (soft foam), about 50 mm (2 inches) thick
▶ scissors
▶ glue
▶ empty cereal box
▶ cardboard
▶ sand or pebbles

1. Cut two pads of soft foam sponge the width of a cereal box.

2. Glue the pads under the two ends of the bottom of a cereal box.

3. Glue the bottom of the pads to a sheet of cardboard.

4. Fill the cereal box with sand or pebbles to give it inertia.

5. Shake the cardboard slightly but quickly and notice how the cereal box remains practically unmoved due to its inertia; it is partially isolated from the cardboard "earth" and returns exactly to its original position.

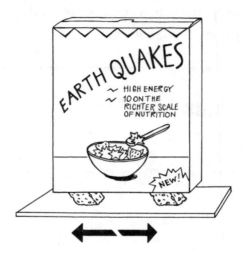

6. Watch as the sponge seen from the side deforms from a rectangle to a *parallelogram* (a shape with the top and bottom edges horizontal and the formerly vertical edges slanted) as the box shakes.

A real building is so heavy that it would completely squash a soft "sponge" isolator. Pads used in real buildings are therefore much stiffer and use a sandwich technique with many alternating layers of hard rubber sheets and steel plates. Many buildings in California and Japan are now protected from earthquake damage by sitting on such pads.

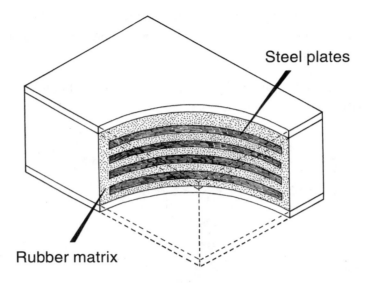

Steel plates

Rubber matrix

Sometimes, when the whole building cannot be isolated (due, for example, to the high expense of doing so), parts of the building or its contents can be isolated by suspending them from the frame of the building. The following experiment will show you how.

A Pendulum Isolator

You'll Need
- ► empty cereal box
- ► scissors
- ► glue
- ► cardboard
- ► heavy thread (called "button and carpet thread")
- ► plastic or cardboard cup
- ► small stick (the size of a match)
- ► sand or pebbles

1. Build a "building structure frame" out of cardboard by first taking an empty cereal box and cutting a window on each of its two long sides.

2. Glue the bottom of the box to a piece of cardboard, representing the earth.

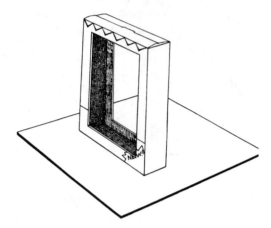

3. Tie the heavy thread to two holes near the top of opposite sides of a plastic or cardboard cup (representing, for instance, a computer that you want to isolate). Hang the cup from the center of the top of the cereal box by tying the thread around a small stick, as shown.

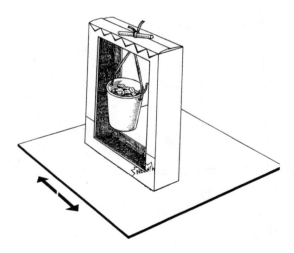

4. Fill the cup with sand or pebbles to give it mass.

5. Shake the cardboard. The frame should move but the hanging cup will remain practically unmoved, like a pendulum, because of its inertia.

Such *hanging isolating systems* have been used in seismic areas to support fragile sculptures in museums as well as heavy boilers in power plants.

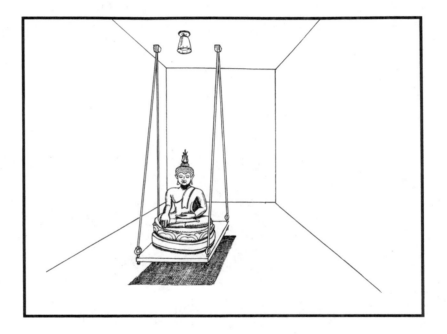

Beginning to tame or fool the earthquakes has given structural engineers a feeling of pride, yet they are still deeply worried about the numerous old buildings that were not designed to resist high seismic forces or by now are so run-down they would not survive a strong quake. Although *retrofitting* (reinforcing of old buildings) is taking place, mostly in hospitals and other especially important structures, this is a complicated process.

Questions

1. Should I run out of my apartment building as soon as I feel an earthquake?

Never—because unless your building were to collapse, you run a much greater risk of getting hurt by something falling from the building facade (like a parapet or an ornament), or by the street traffic, than you would if you crouched under a strong wooden or metal table and held on to its legs. In 1886, a strong earthquake destroyed much of Charleston, South Carolina, and showered stones and bricks on people who had run out to the street seeking safety.

2. I live in the Los Angeles area. Should I ask my family to take precautions against a strong earthquake?

You live in the most severe earthquake zone (zone 4), where the following precautions are recommended to be taken immediately:

- Latch wall and cabinet doors.

- Store emergency supplies of food and other essentials.

- Rehearse with your family the emergency plan you chose to enact in the event of an earthquake.

- Check with school authorities to make sure they have taken similar measures.

You might also suggest to your parents that they take the following additional measures, getting detailed instructions from the local earthquake authorities:

- Anchor any heavy furniture or pieces of equipment (like a chest of drawers, gas water heater, computer, etc.) to the floor or to the studs in the walls, not to partitions that are not firmly attached to the ceiling.

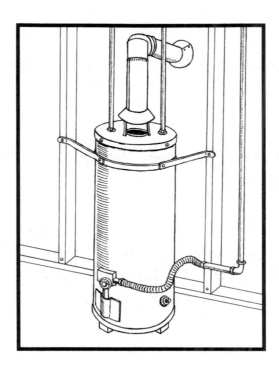

- Securely fasten pictures and other heavy objects hanging on the walls or those resting on the floor.

- Fasten valuable equipment on secure shelves or to anchored tables.

- Have your home or building checked by an engineer to make sure it conforms to the most recent antiseismic code requirements.

3. My dad has an office near the top of a tall skyscraper in San Francisco. Is he safe?

If the Big One comes to San Francisco and is of Richter magnitude 8 or above, your father's high-rise may suffer structural damage but should not collapse. The 1992 Loma Prieta earthquake of Richter magnitude 7.1 did not damage any high-rises.

4. My mother told me that Japanese hotels have instructions for their guests in case of an earthquake. What are they?

The instructions—which, incidentally, are valid anywhere in the world—are:

- Turn off electric appliances (TV, radio, stove, etc.).

- Stay away from windows.

- Crouch under a desk or table to protect your head against falling objects.

- Unlock doors (in case you have to leave in a hurry).

These suggestions are given in case of a serious earthquake. The Japanese take everyday mild earthquakes in stride.

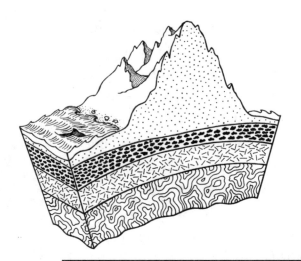

The Smoking Mountains

You've already learned that earthquakes and volcanoes are closely related. You might even say that they are cousins, each with their own personality. Earthquakes are secretive and impetuous, acting suddenly and without warning; volcanoes have a more deliberate and show-offy nature, winding up for an eruption and then spitting up *lava* (red-hot melted rock) for all of us to hear, see, and smell. Yes, there is often the smell of rotten eggs at the time of an eruption, from a chemical called *sulfur dioxide.*

Not all volcanoes behave the same way. Some may be gentle, such as Mauna Loa on Hawaii or Mount Etna on Sicily, pouring hot lava out of their *craters* (the holes at the top of volcanic mountains) so slowly that people can watch and walk away. Others may be violent, such as Mount Vesuvius near Naples, Italy, or Mount St. Helens in the western United States, suddenly exploding and hurling *bombs* (big boulders), *lapilli* (small stones), and lava dust high into the air and rapidly down the face of the conical mountain—so fast that people don't have time to get out of the way. But, unlike earthquakes, all volcanoes give warning of an impending eruption by rumbling and blowing off steam.

Volcanoes got their name from Vulcan, the Roman god of fire, forge, and hearth, whose "hot" festival was held on one of the hottest days of the year (in the Northern Hemisphere), August 23. Volcanoes are born wherever the tremendous pressure of the earth's crust pushes the thick, soupy magma of the mantle through cracks in the crust up to the earth's surface as flowing,

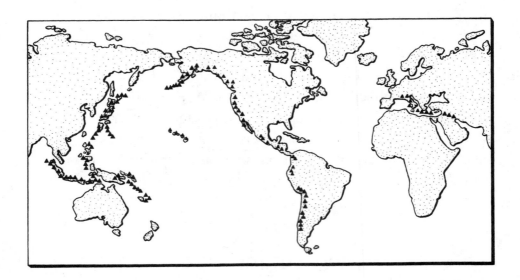

flaming, slow-moving rivers of lava, or violent eruptions spewing rocks and lava dust into the air. Since this happens mostly along the boundaries of the slow-moving tectonic plates (see p. 3), there is an obvious relationship between the earth-shaking quakes and the lava-spewing volcanoes. In the United States, for example, most volcanoes are found along the West Coast, where our strongest earthquakes also occur. They are found as well all around the edge of the Pacific Ocean, called the *Ring of Fire*, and along the same strip from Portugal to Australia where earthquakes occur. Compare the map on p. 12 to the map on the facing page to prove this to yourself.

A Spewing Volcano

If you want to build your own volcano and excite a volcanic eruption, the ideal location is either in the sandlot of a playground or, even better, on a sandy beach, where you can build a more substantial volcano with wet sand. If you can't get outside, you can also build a cardboard volcano at home or in school as described on p. 110.

You'll Need
- pill or film container, at least 50 mm (2 in.) tall (the taller the better)
- sand (or cardboard, if working outside)
- measuring spoons
- baking soda
- liquid soap or detergent
- red wine vinegar

1. Get an empty round plastic pill or film container, as shown.

2. Build a conic mountain of sand. (If you are making a volcano inside, you may instead build the cone of the volcano with cardboard and cut a hole at the top to fit in the pill container. See p. 110 to learn how this is done.)

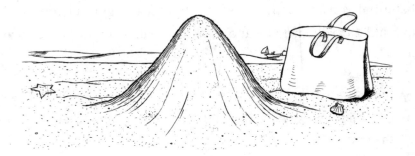

3. Push the pill container into the top of the volcano so that it's flush with the top, thus opening a "crater" in it. (If you're using the cardboard volcano, push down the pill container to fit tightly into the center hole, flush with the cardboard "crater." Tape it in place if needed.)

4. Pour a heaping half-teaspoon of baking soda into the pill container and then add a few drops of liquid soap or detergent on top of it. Then fill the container with red wine vinegar.

5. A foamy "lava" will spew from the crater and flow down the side of the volcano for a while, longer with a larger pill container. The "lava" erupts because the vinegar is an *acid* and when chemically combined with the baking soda, which is a *base*, it makes *carbon dioxide*, a colorless gas that fills the soap with bubbles and pushes out the "lava."

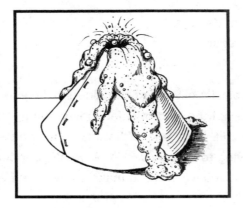

There are many volcanoes on the surface of the earth. At present about five hundred are *active*, or alive, and many more are *extinct*, or dead. The *dormant*, or sleeping, volcanoes are by far the most dangerous form of active volcano, because they may sleep for centuries and wake up unexpectedly at any time. Mount Pinatubo in the Philippines had been dormant for six hundred years before local seismologists began to measure seismic activity in 1991. It erupted violently two weeks later, devastating a wide area not far from the Philippine capital of Manila and killing nine hundred people.

Another Volcanic Eruption

Because of the messy nature of this eruption, this experiment should only be done outdoors or in an area that can be easily cleaned up.

You'll Need
- pill or film container, at least 50 mm (2 in.) tall (the taller the better)
- pill or film container lid
- sand (or cardboard, if working inside)
- measuring spoons
- baking soda
- liquid soap or detergent
- red wine vinegar

1. Check the plastic pill or film container: make sure the lid of the container is not the kind of safety cover that makes it hard for a child to open it, but the kind that fits tightly on the container without having to be screwed in place. (If your container has a safety cover, you will have to make a new one: get a cork from a

wine bottle and wrap it with aluminum foil until it is the same diameter as the container and will fit tight.)

2. Build the same volcano as described in the Spewing Volcano experiment (see p. 105).

3. To excite a volcanic eruption, tightly close the pill container with its cover immediately after you pour the vinegar into it.

4. The expansion of the gaseous carbon dioxide should create enough pressure in the container to shoot the cover high into the air, together with drops of the brownish mixture of red wine vinegar, liquid soap, and baking soda. It is a dramatic show that, besides shooting up the container cover and spray mixture, also makes a loud popping sound.

WARNING: Stand away from the eruption so that the top of the pill container doesn't hit you.

Since the earth's crust is thinnest under the oceans (see p. 2), you should not be surprised to learn that 90 percent of the earth's volcanic eruptions occur at the bottom of the sea, creating ocean ridges (see p. 11) and, at times, generating horrendous tsunamis (see p. 27). A thousand volcanoes, large and small, have been recently discovered in a relatively small area of the South Pacific.

Build a Cardboard Volcano

You'll Need
▶ sheet of flexible cardboard (such as a shirt insert), about 200 by 350 mm (8 by 14 in.)
▶ large compass, radius of at least 200 mm (8 in.)
▶ scissors
▶ stapler
▶ paints (optional)

1. Take a large compass and place the point in one corner of a sheet of flexible cardboard. Draw an arc from the short to the long side, as shown. (If you do not have a compass large enough to draw the circle, make a compass by tying a pencil to one end of a piece of string that is tied on the other end to a pin at the corner of the cardboard. Adjust the distance between the pin and the pencil so that it is 200 millimeters [8 inches] long by moving the knot tied around the pencil.)

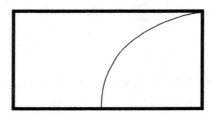

2. Place the point of the compass at the spot where the arc intersects the long side, and draw an arc that intersects the other short side, as shown. From that point to the center of the arc, draw a straight line.

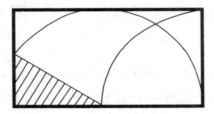

3. Cut the cardboard sheet around the perimeter of the partial circle.

4. Draw a circle at the center of the partial circle, about the size of the diameter of the pill container, and cut radial lines from the center to the perimeter of this small circle. Slightly bend down the radial segments.

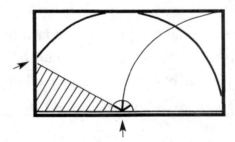

5. Bend the cardboard into a cone overlapping the shaded triangle shown above and staple it together.

6. You may want to decorate your volcano by painting on its surface light green fields of grass, dark green trees, flows of gray lava, and black rocks.

7. Make the volcano erupt or explode according to the instructions in the previous two experiments, but do it in a kitchen or bathroom, where you can easily clean up the mess caused by the eruption.

So far you have only heard of volcanoes' destructive powers, but it would be unfair not to stress the essential role volcanoes have played and still play in the life of the earth. When the earth was formed about five billion years ago, volcanoes were everywhere, and by pouring their lava over the earth's surface, they helped to build up the crust on which we live. They then helped to generate the atmosphere of carbon dioxide, steam, and other vapors that made possible the life of plants and animals on earth, the only planet of our solar system that deserves to be called "the life planet."

Once volcanoes become inactive and the lava they have spilled on the earth's surface breaks up over thousands of years into small grains, the result is some of the most fertile soil on earth.

A Smoking Volcano

You'll Need
- adult helper
- soil or moist sand
- shovel
- stick
- paper
- kindling wood

► matches
► newspaper
► cardboard volcano (from previous experiment; optional)
► dry ice (optional)
► towel or prongs (optional)
► small bowl of water (optional)

1. Build a large outdoor mound (your volcano) out of soil or moist sand using a shovel or your hands.

2. Open a horizontal tunnel at its base all the way to its center under the crater, and enlarge it into a cave, as shown.

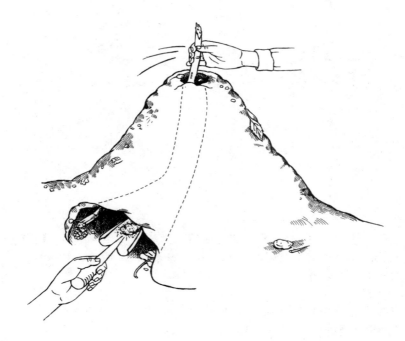

3. With a stick, pierce a vertical hole from the top of the cone down to the cave.

4. Push some moist paper through the side tunnel into the cave and put some kindling on top of it.

5. With the help of an adult, set the kindling on fire using a lit rolled-up newspaper or a long match. The volcano should blow white-gray smoke out of the crater.

6. You can also create a smoking mountain indoors. Cut a hole in the side of your cardboard cone (see p. 110) and set it on a kitchen counter.

7. Remove the pill container and fold back the radial segments slightly to close off the top of the cone.

8. Get a piece of dry ice from a drugstore or ice cream shop. **WARNING:** Don't hold the dry ice with your fingers as they may stick tightly to the ice and suffer a painful injury! Use a towel or prongs to place it in a dish of water and push it into the cave of your cardboard volcano. It will blow white "smoke" for a while.

Dry ice is frozen carbon dioxide, the same colorless gas obtained by mixing vinegar and baking soda. It freezes at a very low temperature and condenses the humidity or vapor in the air into a white cloud that looks like smoke.

Volcanoes can also be used as a source of energy. The island of Ischia in the Gulf of Naples is one of the places on earth dotted with a large number of *fumaroles*, vents in the ground from which steam has been escaping for hundreds of thousands of years. The fumaroles are small cracks in the earth's crust that allow underground water to reach the deep rocks heated by the magma. The heated rocks cause underground water to evaporate into steam, which the Ischian farmers use to warm their tomato plants in winter.

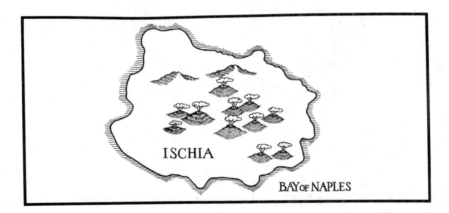

In more recent times the same steam from heated underground water has been exploited for industrial purposes in *geothermal installations*. The first large geothermal energy installation in the world was built in 1904 at Larderello in Tuscany, Italy. Recently expanded, it is still in use today. It consists of a series of *steam turbines*, engines similar to windmills but turned not by the air but by hot steam obtained from the upper layer of the earth's crust. The turbines are connected to *electric generators*, the rotating machinery that creates electric power. The Larderello, together with an adjoining geothermal plant, serves the power needs of a large local area and replaces generators run with oil-fed engines, thus saving Italy the need of importing one million tons of costly foreign oil a year.

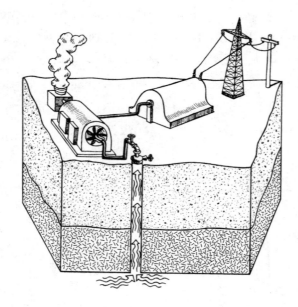

In 1995, 1 percent of the electric power in the United States was supplied by geothermal sources (in California and the Midwest). In the near future, 10 percent of the United States needs may be met by such sources. Meanwhile, the search for new sources of geothermal energy is going on all over the world.

Geothermal Energy

Build you own model of a geothermal installation.

You'll Need
▶ adult helper
▶ aluminum foil
▶ dowel or stick, 25 mm (1 in.) diameter
▶ rubber band
▶ tea kettle with spout
▶ water
▶ small windmill connected to an electric generator and a small electric bulb (Tinkertoy has such a windmill connected with a chain to the shaft of a generator, which you can buy at a toy store, or see "Resources," p. 131, for other possibilities)

1. Form aluminum foil into a tube about 25 millimeters (1 inch) in diameter by wrapping it around a stick, folding over the seams and then removing the stick.

2. Attach the aluminum foil tube with a rubber band to the spout of a kettle, with the aluminum tube pointing out horizontally.

3. Fill the kettle with water and, with an adult's help, bring the water to a high boil so that the steam blows from the kettle spout at high speed. **WARNING:** To avoid being burned, do not place any part of your body in the path of the steam.

4. Place the windmill in front of the tube so that the blowing steam will make it turn.

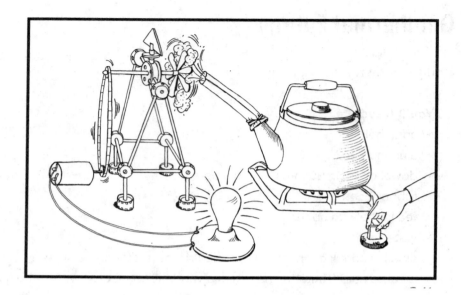

5. Switch the generator on and the little bulb should light up.

Except for the evaporation of the water by the heat of your stove rather than by the heat of the magma, in physical principles your installation is identical to a geothermal installation.

Questions

1. We live in central Arkansas near Hot Springs. Does the presence of hot springs mean that there is a danger of volcanoes?

Hot springs are not indicators of volcanic activity and are actually safety valves that release pressure created when rainwater turns to steam as it seeps down to the hot rocks below the earth's surface. Many hot springs merely flow, while some become *geysers* that erupt periodically, like Old Faithful in Yellowstone National Park.

2. Near our home in Japan is Mount Fuji. It looks so serene with its snowcapped cone. Is there a danger that it will erupt?

Mount Fuji is a dormant volcano that last erupted in 1707. It could erupt at any time, but before it does, it will provide warnings by starting to fume and blow off steam and possibly causing earthquakes.

Conclusion

Earthquakes, volcanoes, and tsunamis are becoming increasingly deadly and costly as they hit more densely populated parts of the world. Since some of us live in regions in which there are active volcanoes or where there is a chance of seismic activity, knowing what to expect and how to guard yourself from harm are two lessons we hope you will take away with you after having read this book.

Appendix

Important Earthquakes, Volcanoes, and Tsunamis

This list is not meant to be complete or definitive. It is simply our choice of those events that had the greatest impact on the people or the history of the time when they occurred. These events are remembered because they forever changed the environment in which we live.

4600 B.C.

In the western United States a chain of volcanoes dot the Cascade Mountains, stretching from northern California to northern Washington. Near the southern end of this chain is a volcano that is known in Native American lore as Mount Mazama. It was the site of one of the largest volcanic eruptions in recorded history. The volcano's cone collapsed to form a depression, or *caldera*, 589 meters (1,932 feet) deep. The caldera filled with water and is today called Crater Lake.

1623 B.C.

The Greek island of Thera (also known as Santorini) is located in the Aegean Sea and is believed to be where the mythical kingdom of Atlantis was located. It was the site of a catastrophic eruption that blew off the volcano's cone, leaving only a partial bowl that is today the island's harbor. As a result of the explosion, volcanic ash buried the island's city of Akrotiri and was carried by the wind as far away as Egypt's Nile Delta and the shore of Turkey. Sailors lost their ships and farmers lost their crops under the same ashfall. So severe were the changes in the environment that the Minoan civilization, an ancient culture that lived on the Aegean island, collapsed and quickly disappeared.

A.D. 79

Mount Vesuvius on the Bay of Naples in Italy is the only currently active volcano in Europe. It was known at the time of the Roman Empire as the site of eruptions since antiquity. In A.D. 79, the Roman towns of Herculaneum and Pompeii at the base of the mountain were totally unprepared for the catastrophic eruption that buried them in a shower of deadly cinders. Both towns were forgotten, hidden under a mountain of mud and ash until rediscovered in the 18th century by workmen digging a new canal.

1755

On November 1, Lisbon, the capital of Portugal, was struck by a disastrous earthquake with an estimated Richter magnitude of 8.7.

It caused almost all of the city's buildings to topple and a tsunami to roll into the harbor from the ocean, throwing boats onto the land and drowning thousands of the city's inhabitants. After the earth had stopped shaking and the waters from the ocean wave had receded, fires broke out all over the city, totally destroying it. Within a few years the city was rebuilt around a new central square, the Terreiro do Paço.

1815

Lying along the rim of the Pacific Ocean in the Ring of Fire, and facing the Indian Ocean to their west, are the islands of Indonesia. They compose one of the most active volcanic areas on earth, with more than 80 active volcanoes. On the Indonesian island of Sumbawa, there occurred one of the largest eruptions in recent times. A huge quantity of ash was thrown into the atmosphere. This ash then circled the earth for the next few years, causing major changes in the weather. In Europe, crops failed because summer never arrived. In the northeastern United States, it snowed in June, and in the South, there was frost on the Fourth of July.

1883

Because there are so many active volcanoes on the Indonesian islands, it is not surprising that the region was host to another great eruption when the island volcano called Krakatau blew up and disappeared under the ocean. The tsunami it caused moved across the Pacific Ocean and killed thousands of people on adjacent islands.

1906

The city of San Francisco lies on one of the longest cracks in the earth, the San Andreas Fault. This fault extends virtually the whole length of the state of California. Early on the morning of April 18, part of the crack around San Francisco ripped open, violently shaking the earth with a Richter magnitude of 8.3, knocking down chimneys and brick walls, bursting underground water and gas pipes, and twisting the city's streetcar tracks like pretzels. A series of fires that started after the earthquake caused even greater damage and burned one-third of the city.

1908

The island of Sicily at the foot of Italy is dominated by Mount Etna. Like most of Italy, the island lies in the Alpide belt, a region of heavy seismic activity. The town of Messina, on the tip of the island facing the Italian mainland, was struck by the worst quake ever recorded in the country. The quake, of Richter magnitude 7.5, killed over 120,000 people, most of whom were trapped in the rubble of their masonry houses. Mount Etna is an active volcano that constantly threatens the heavily populated, fertile lands at its base. It last erupted in 2001.

1923

The Japanese are used to feeling the earth shake beneath them, since their homeland is constantly being struck by earthquakes, most of moderate intensity but some strong. Just before lunchtime on September 1, Tokyo, the capital of Japan, was hit by a powerful earthquake of Richter magnitude 8.3. It toppled thousands of lightly built houses, threw down brick walls, caused some buildings to sink into liquefied soil, and gave rise to a tsunami that roared in from Tokyo Bay, washing out bridges and riverside houses. Over a hundred thousand people died because of the quake and from the fires that sprang up immediately thereafter and burned down most of the city.

1964

The strongest earthquake ever to strike the North American continent occurred in the sparsely populated region around Anchorage, Alaska, on Good Friday. Compared to most quakes, which last less than a minute, it was one of the longest-lasting ones, with a duration of almost three minutes. The 8.4 Richter magnitude quake flattened buildings and, because of soil liquefaction, caused houses to topple down hills. It opened cracks in the ground, caused rock slides and *mud spouts* (where mud shoots up out of the ground like a geyser), and spawned a tsunami off the Pacific Ocean that was responsible for most of the few casualties.

1976

In the last three thousand years, it is estimated that China has suffered the loss of over 13,000,000 inhabitants to earthquakes. For this reason, the Chinese have pioneered methods of predicting earthquakes and have achieved some success. For instance, in the province of Liaoning in 1975, people were given warning of an impending quake in time to allow them to leave their homes. But one year later, in the middle of the night, a huge quake of Richter magnitude 7.9 hit the town of Tangshan without warning, trapping thousands of people in collapsing houses and killing an estimated three hundred thousand people.

1995

A deadly earthquake occurred quite unexpectedly on a January morning in Kobe, Japan. For years Japanese scientists had predicted that a quake would strike the region southwest of Tokyo. They were taken completely by surprise when a 7.2 Richter magnitude quake hit Kobe, a city southwest of Osaka, almost 420 kilometers (260 miles) away from Tokyo. The Kobe quake caused great damage and loss of life. An elevated roadway in the center of the city fell over on its side as if pushed by a giant hand. Some buildings were squashed, and the port area was a shambles, with huge cracks in piers and fallen structures everywhere. As with most quakes in modern cities, fires erupted as a result of gas leaking from broken pipes. The overall damage proved it to be the most costly natural disaster ever.

2004

Where there are volcanoes, there is usually seismic activity, and such is the case in the Indonesian islands. On the day after Christmas, the most powerful earthquake in the past 40 years, with a Richter magnitude of 9.0, struck in the ocean bed off the west coast of Sumatra, Indonesia. It was so strong that the whole planet shook, the North Pole shifted by several centimeters, the length of a day was shortened by 3 microseconds, and earthquakes were initiated as far away as Alaska.

Although the earthquake was exceptionally strong, no buildings were toppled and few people were hurt by it directly, because it was sufficiently far away from inhabited areas. However, the earthquake resulted in a 10 meter (30 foot) shift (sideward sliding) along a 1,000 kilometer (600 mile) subduction boundary along which the ocean bed was also lifted by several meters. This triggered a series of devastating tsunamis that traveled across the Indian Ocean and caused flooding and death in 11 countries including Indonesia, Sri Lanka, India, Thailand, and Myanmar. The tsunami waves that arrived along those shores were as much as 15 meters (50 feet) high; they smashed everything in their path, drowning almost a quarter million people.

To understand how this single earthquake sent a shock across the globe, hold a soccer ball in your hand and have a friend hit the outside of the ball with a book. Notice that the force of the impact travels through the ball and into your hands. Also notice that the harder your friend hits the ball, the more vibrations you feel. This is what happened across the planet as a result of the Sumatra quake.

2005

Kashmir, a region along the foothills of the Himalayan Mountains, is both part of northern Pakistan and India. It is a rugged land with many small mountain villages connected by narrow hillside roads—and, more significantly, it lies along the boundary between the Indian and Eurasian tectonic plates, and is therefore in a region of seismic activity. As it has for about one hundred thousand years, the Indian plate continues to slip under the Eurasian plate, causing the

Himalayas to rise ever higher. Experts had long predicted that a major quake was likely, since there had not been one in the region for a hundred years, and a great deal of energy was stored along the rough boundary between the plates.

On the morning of October 8, as children were just starting their school day, the earth began to suddenly shake with an earthquake of Richter magnitude 7.6. The quake was centered near the city of Muzaffarabad, and it resulted in people being buried as schools collapsed, houses crumbled, and even a 19-story building partly collapsed in Islamabad, 100 kilometers (60 miles) from the epicenter. Landslides blocked many mountain roads, isolating villages and preventing aid from reaching them as winter approached. Over 80,000 people were killed and over three million people were left homeless as their concrete block homes were reduced to piles of rubble. The quake was felt as far away as Kabul, the capital of Afghanistan, 670 kilometers (400 miles) to the west. In parts of India and Bangladesh, *seiches* (which is what happens when water in a lake sloshes back and forth) were observed.

2008

India was an island until about 50 million years ago, when it started moving toward and eventually crashed into the Eurasian tectonic plate. Even today, it is still moving at a snail's pace of about 50 millimeters (2 inches) per year, further raising the Himalayan mountains and pushing up the Tibetan plateau. As a result, earthquakes occur near the South China border, from Burma to Afghanistan. On the afternoon of May 12, along the mountainous boundary of Sichuan province of China, an earthquake of Richter magnitude 7.9 devastated the region, collapsing buildings and causing upward of 20,000 deaths. It was the worst earthquake in the country since the 1976 Tangshan quake.

Resources

There are numerous resources available on the Internet that you can explore to find more information on earthquakes, volcanoes, and tsunamis. Some sites that offer additional explanations, photos, access to experimental materials, etc. include:

- **National Geographic—Science and Space:** Videos and photos.
  http://science.nationalgeographic.com/science/earth/natural-disasters/earthquake-profile.html

- **Scholastic Science Interactives:** Questions, answers, and projects.
  http://teacher.scholastic.com/activities/science/earthquake_interactives.htm

- **The Science Spot:** Links to many other sites including the USGS, animations, scientific fair project ideas, and pictures
  www.sciencespot.net/Pages/kdzethsci2.html

- **42eXplore:** Resource for experiments.
  www.42explore.com/quakes.htm

- **Kazoo Toys:** Purchase the Earthquake & Volcanoes Science Kit by Thames & Kosmos.
  www.kazootoys.com/eavoexkit.html

- **Langleys Toys:** Purchase a Loopwing Wind Power Generator Set with electric car; can be used in the Geothermal Energy experiment (see p. 117).
  www.langleystoys.com/acatalog/science_sets.html

- **Neatstuff Collectibles:** Purchase a steam power plant, generator, and light.
  www.neatstuff.net/wilesco-steam.html

If you want to know even more about the scientific story behind earthquakes and volcanoes, see the book *Why the Earth Quakes* by Matthys Levy and Mario Salvadori (W. W. Norton, 1993).

Index